Religion and *Morality*

GCSE Religious Studies for **AQA B**

Lesley Parry,
Jan Hayes and Kim Hands

HODDER
EDUCATION
AN HACHETTE UK COMPANY

Acknowledgements

Thanks go to our friends who made the tea and listened to the discussions and arguments! Kim wants to thank her family, and the Scrabble world. We hope this book will go a long way to helping young people get to grips with the topics. Good luck in your exams.

Photo credits

The Publishers would like to thank the following for permission to reproduce copyright material:
Cover © Benjamin Lowy/Corbis; **p.5** Rex Features/Everett Collection; **p.6** Science Photo Library/AJ Photo; **p.10** *t* Science Photo Library/Dr. Yorgos Nikas, *b* Roslin Institute/University of Edinburgh; **p.12** *t* NHS Blood and Transplant, *b* National Health Service; **p.18** *all* © Lesley Parry; **p.22** Help the Hospices; **p.23** *all* St Ann's hospice; **p.25** PA Photos; **p.30** *ct* Science Photo Library/Geoff Tompkinson, *cb* Science Photo Library/AJ Photo; **p.34** *t* Corbis/Gideon Mendel, *b* PA Photos/Chris Young; **p.37** *t* Alamy/Kuttig-People, *c* Department of Health, *b* Action on Smoking and Health; **p.38** *t* © Lesley Parry, *b* Alamy/Lightworks Media; **p.39** Alcohol Concern; **p.41** Release; **p.43** © Lesley Parry; **p.44** *t* Alamy/Andrew Woodley, *b* Alamy/Radius Images; **p.45** *t* Alamy/Steve Bloom, *b* Alamy/Itani; **p.46** *t* Corbis/David Ribinger, *b* Alamy/ArkReligion.com; **p.52** *t* Alamy/Workingwales, *b* PA Photos/Toby Melville; **p.53** Rex Features/Richard Gardner; **p.56** *l* Corbis/Mark Jenkinson, *r* Corbis/Brooks Kraft/Sygma; **p.57** Amnesty International UK; **p.64** *l* Rex Features/Ben Alcraft, *c* Rex Features/Dennis Closon, *r* PA Photos/Andrew Milligan; **p.65** *tl* PA Photos/Rebecca Naden, *tc* PA Photos/Tony Marshall/Empics Sport, *tr* PA Photos/Owen Humphreys, *bl* PA Photos/Heiko Wolfraum/DPA, *br* PA Photos/Danny Lawson; **p.68** *tl* Hodder Education, *tr* Alamy/Eyebyte, *bl* Alamy/Steven May; **p.72** *tc* Shelter, *tr* Rex Features/Alisdair MacDonald, *bl* The Salvation Army; **p.74** *t* Alamy/Alex Segre, *b* PA Photos/Adam Davy/Empics Sport; **p.78** *tl* PA Photos/Eranga Jayawardena/AP, *cl* © Lesley Parry, *cr* Rex Features/Paul Grover, *tr* PA Photos/Pavel Rahman/AP; **p.80** *l* Corbis Karen Kasmauski, *c* Rex Features/Sutton-Hibbert, *r* Corbis/John Carnemolla/Australian Picture Library; **p.81** *t* PA Photos/Adam Butler/AP, *b* PA Photos/Eranga Jayawardena/AP; **p.82** Marcus Lyon/Fairtrade Foundation; **p.83** *tl* Corbis/Paulo Fridman, *tr* PA Photos/Andy Wong/AP, *bl* PA Photos/Glenna Gordon/AP; **p.84** *l* Tibet Foundation, *c* CAFOD, *r* Sewa International; **p.85** *l* Reproduced with permission of Islamic Relief Worldwide, *c* World Jewish Relief, *r* Khalsa Aid; **p.86** Rex Features; **p.88** *l* Village Volunteers/www.villagevolunteers.org, *r* Rainforest Alliance; **p.97** © Lesley Parry; **p.98** © Lesley Parry; **p.99** Rex Features/Paul Grover.

Every effort has been made to trace all copyright holders, but if any have been inadvertently overlooked the Publishers will be pleased to make the necessary arrangements at the first opportunity.

Words highlighted in **bold** are defined in the Glossary on p.100.

Although every effort has been made to ensure that website addresses are correct at time of going to press, Hodder Education cannot be held responsible for the content of any website mentioned in this book. It is sometimes possible to find a relocated web page by typing in the address of the home page for a website in the URL window of your browser.

Hachette UK's policy is to use papers that are natural, renewable and recyclable products and made from wood grown in sustainable forests. The logging and manufacturing processes are expected to conform to the environmental regulations of the country of origin.

Orders: please contact Bookpoint Ltd, 130 Milton Park, Abingdon, Oxon OX14 4SB. Telephone: +44 (0)1235 827720. Fax: +44 (0)1235 400454. Lines are open 9.00–5.00, Monday to Saturday, with a 24-hour message answering service. Visit our website at www.hoddereducation.co.uk.

© Lesley Parry, Jan Hayes and Kim Hands 2009
First published in 2009 by
Hodder Education,
An Hachette UK company
338 Euston Road
London NW1 3BH

Impression number   5 4 3
Year   2013 2012 2011 2010

Illustrations by Oxford Illustrators and Richard Duszczak
Typeset in 11pt Minion by DC Graphic Design Ltd, Swanley Village, Kent
Printed in Italy

A catalogue record for this title is available from the British Library

ISBN 978 0 340 98366 9

Contents page

Topic Four Religious attitudes to crime and punishment 49

Topic Five Religious attitudes to rich and poor in British society 64

Topic Six Religious attitudes to world poverty 78

Appendix I Revision guide

Appendix II What a question paper looks like

Glossary

Index

Introduction

This book has been written specifically to meet the AQA Specification B Unit 3 syllabus. It follows the Unit outline, moving through the topics in the order of the Unit as set out in the specification. It is informed additionally by the specification from which it grew (also called Specification B).

The Unit is examined through one exam paper of one hour and thirty minutes. All six topics within the Unit will be represented on that paper, though candidates will be required to answer questions on only four topics. Each question is worth 18 marks, and with quality of written response now within the mark scheme itself (rather than an additional sum), the total for the paper will be 72 marks. An example of the paper and what it should look like is found in Appendix II at the back of this book. This is annotated to help demystify the exam language and paper style.

This Unit, when studied in conjunction with a second Unit leads to a full GCSE qualification.

The topic sections within the book cover the Unit content from a variety of angles, as well as providing the necessary information required by those studying for the exam. Each topic asks students to think about what they are being told, and about the implications of the issues. There are many opportunities for evaluation work, which now forms 50 per cent of the total mark for the exam. Knowledge and understanding of the topics are important, but ability to apply that knowledge is vital to gain the highest grades. The style of text is designed to encourage and develop exactly that.

Teachers often find it difficult to judge how much time to give to the varying elements of a topic. Experience of exams helps teachers work out what can and can't be reasonably asked on each topic. In this book, a rule of thumb could be to look at how much space is given to any element of a topic. If it is a page, then really it needs to be covered thoroughly, whereas a short paragraph indicates that there is a limit to what can be asked, and so less depth is needed. It isn't a firm rule, but is helpful guidance to bear in mind.

Exam technique is a constant theme, as it can cost candidates many marks if poor. It is worth taking the class time to teach/learn good technique via the mechanics of good answers. The authors of this book are all senior examiners with AQA, and have lengthy experience in their roles. They give good advice, so make good use of it!

The specification allows centres to prepare candidates to answer from one or more religious traditions on any question. This book allows study of a single religious tradition, or of several – all religious traditions are commented on for each element within each topic.

Given this is an issues course; students should be encouraged to collect their own examples of the issues as met in the news. They can collect, add comments, give their own opinion, and even try to say what they think religion(s) would say. This will help with their recall and provide real examples to call on in the exam.

A revision outline in Appendix I is designed to support revision, but can act as a checklist for students as they move through the course.

About this course

This course gets you to think about six key modern day issues. Some of them will have directly affected you, or you will have direct experience of them. Some you will know of through other people's experience. Some you may only know of through the media. Keep in mind that you already have a whole load of knowledge about these issues, and you can use that in your exam. Your knowledge on the topics of this exam is probably greater than in any other GCSE you are studying, because it is such a topical exam, with ideas close to the experience of young people. Be confident, and use what you know.

It's a Religious Studies exam, so you have to know the attitude of at least one religion to these topics. Some schools study just one, which stops students confusing ideas of several religions. Others study two, which makes it easier to get to the higher marks in the exam, because there is more to say. Whatever your school does, make sure you learn the religious bits – they are as exam-friendly as possible in this book. You can't get beyond about a D grade without knowing any religious stuff.

For the exam, you have to answer questions on four of the topics. All six topics will always be on the exam paper – you just answer questions on four. Actually, you could answer more, because they'll still get marked, and the four best answered questions get taken forward as your marks. BUT – people who do this, often don't get great marks. It is only ever a good idea if you have finished answering – at *your* right speed (not having rushed) – and still have loads of time left. If you are one of those people who has lots of time left in an exam, then why not do another question? You have nothing to lose, and potentially something to gain.

As you go through the issues, you will have opinions and attitudes to them. That is good! You will be asked about your own opinion to many of the issues as part of the exam. So do take the chances to discuss and explain your own opinions – it helps you present them better in the exam when you have to.

What do I think?

Religious attitudes to matters of life (medical ethics)

Religious attitudes to the elderly and death

Religious attitudes to drug abuse

Religious attitudes to crime and punishment

Religious attitudes to rich and poor in British society

Religious attitudes to world poverty

Keep your eye on the news – there will be lots of stories which link to these issues in the time it takes to do this course. Those stories could figure in exam papers, which are written about fifteen months before you get to sit the exam, and often use topical stories. They certainly give you a bigger range of examples to use in your answers when you are trying to explain or back up a point you make. Could be time to start a scrapbook?!

The religious bit...

Religion also has opinions on those issues. This is a Religious Studies course, after all, so you are going to see the attitudes of some religions. You will have to write about them in the exam, if you want to get good grades. That means trying to understand what those attitudes are, and where they come from; in other words, the beliefs and teachings of the religions. In this book, you'll be given a small number of beliefs and teachings for each religion on each topic. Quite often you can use these teachings in a few different topics (which always helps!). If a teaching will apply to more than one topic – use it.

This double page gives you some general teachings, which you can apply to all the different topics. It cuts down the number of teachings you have to learn, and means you understand these quite strongly. However, the best answers in exams always use beliefs and teachings that are specific to the topics, as well as the general ones. Don't forget to learn some of those when you meet them later, as well. Mark this page, or copy these teachings into the front of your book or file. Then use them as the basis for your work. When you study a topic, refer back to these to help you work out what the attitude will be to that topic.

Buddhism ☸

1 Reincarnation and karma – our words, thoughts and deeds create energies which shape our future rebirths. We need to make sure these are positive.
2 The Five Precepts, (guidelines for living). These are – not harming others (ahimsa); using language kindly; not taking what is not freely given; not clouding our minds; no sexual misconduct.
3 **Compassion** (loving kindness).

Christianity ✝

1 Jesus' two key teachings – love God; love your neighbour.
2 Equality of all, because in Genesis we are told that God made each of us.
3 Justice (fairness) – since everyone is equal, everyone deserves fairness.
4 Forgiveness and love are ideas taught by Jesus, and are shown in his actions.

Hinduism ॐ

Hindu holy books list many virtues. These include:

1 ahimsa (non-violence)
2 self-discipline
3 tolerance
4 service to others
5 compassion
6 providing shelter/support to others
7 respect for all life
8 wisdom
9 honesty with others and oneself
10 cleanliness.

Islam ☾★

1 The Ummah – brotherhood of all Muslims. This means that all Muslims are equal, and deserve equal respect and treatment.
2 That everyone has to follow duties set by Allah (God), for example, the Five Pillars.
3 Shari'ah law, which is Muslim law stemming from the Qur'an and Hadith, and applied to modern life by Islamic scholars.

Judaism ♇

The Ten Commandments, which are found in the book of Genesis in the Torah:

1 Love only G-d.
2 Make no idols of G-d.
3 Do not take G-d's name in vain.
4 Keep the Sabbath holy.
5 Respect your parents.
6 Do not kill.
7 Do not steal.
8 Do not commit adultery.
9 Do not tell lies.
10 Do not be jealous of what others have.

Sikhism ☬

The Khalsa vows:

1 Meditation and service to the One God, including worship, following the teachings, and wearing the 5Ks as a mark of the faith and devotion to it.
2 Do not use intoxicants.
3 Do not eat meat that has been ritually slaughtered (most Sikhs are vegetarians).
4 Equality of all people, leading to respect for all and a desire to fight injustice, and including not hurting others by theft or deed.

Sikh ethical virtues – sharing with others, including tithing (sewa); dutifulness; prudence; justice; tolerance; temperance; chastity; patience; contentment; detachment and humility.

Topic One Religious attitudes to matters of life (medical ethics)

This topic is about life – just like it says. It focuses on the beginning of life, and on maintaining life. So there are two very distinct halves to it, and you need to understand the two halves separately. The religion binds it all together because it gives you an idea of the attitudes that religions have to life, and from that you can work out the rights and responsibilities humans have regarding life. For some people, this is a frightening topic because it seems to have lots of science in it, and a lot of people don't find understanding science easy or comfortable. In this book, let's make it simple – you are studying religion, and only need the most basic knowledge of the science. Don't worry – you'll be fine…

Task

Have a look at these topics – with a partner, work out what you know or have heard. You will know lots about each from what you hear in the news, or from the experience of your family and friends. You may know information from science lessons, where you have studied the science of the topics. They may be things you have never heard of, but your partner has. Share your knowledge.

Beginnings of life

Fertility treatments – IVF

AID

AIH

Surrogacy

Maintaining life

Genetic engineering

Embryology

Stem cell research/technology

Cloning

Transplant surgery

Blood transfusion

Now you should have a working definition of each or most, anyway.

> Can you think why we might want to keep any of them as part of our medical system?
> Can you think of why we should be wary of any of them as part of our medical system?

Those questions are crucial. The exam might ask you what these different things are – if it does, then it will probably only be for a small number of marks. However, it is more likely to ask you what the benefits and issues of each are, because that is where the religion and ethics come in (and this is a religion and ethics exam!). It is most likely to ask you what religions think about them, which is a mix of the benefits and issues with religious teachings. We will do all of that in the next few pages.

Now you know the elements of this topic

Ethical issues and religious attitudes

Religious people need to make a judgement on what they can or can't do/use. They often have to ask the questions that are on this page. In the exam, when you are asked about religious attitudes to something, use these as starters for the points you make.

Why is life sacred?

It is important to remember that all religions believe that life is sacred and special. This is either because it is created by God as the most important part of the whole creation, or because it is one part of a long journey to enlightenment.

Who has the right to create life?

The fact that humans can now create life without having sexual intercourse is viewed differently depending on religious beliefs. For some religious people, the *only* way to a pregnancy should be sexual intercourse. This means it has been created by God through the act of sex. For some, helping a couple become pregnant is fine, as long as only the couple's egg and sperm are used. This means that scientific methods are acceptable, but any use of donors is not. For others, medical science is seen as a gift of God, or an alleviation of suffering – so it is always acceptable, even when donors are involved.

What about maintaining life – whose right is that?

Well, God created life and gave man **stewardship** and dominion over his creation, according to many religions. So God must permit scientific knowledge and medicine as part of humanity looking after life. If a religious person believes in rebirth or reincarnation, then they would see medicine as helping people and easing suffering – both of which are important. So when we talk about whether it is OK for humans to maintain life through **blood transfusion** and transplantation, then most religious people would say it was.

What about 'Frankenstein technologies'?

Frankenstein was a doctor from a famous story, written by Mary Shelley. He created a human from the body parts of dead humans, and then brought it to life using electricity. The result was a monster. Some religious people see some of the medical technologies as being like what Frankenstein did, and therefore, wrong. Things like **cloning** are seen as man taking God's place. There is also the worry about whether clones can have a soul. Some people believe that **stem cell technology** and embryo research mean that the potential life (the embryo created in a laboratory) doesn't deserve the same respect or rights as an embryo in the womb, or as a person. Each of those technologies means that many embryos are simply discarded or destroyed – and that is bad, because it can be seen as killing, or at the very least disrespecting life!

The Basics

1 Explain what is meant by IVF, AID, AIH and surrogacy.
2 What are the positives about fertility treatment?
3 Can you work out some of the problems to do with fertility treatment? Use the information on page 6 to add to what you can work out for yourself.
4 **Fertility treatment is an expensive waste of money.** What do you think? Explain your opinion.

Now you have thought about some of the ethics

Science starting life

Having children is part of nature. Many couples feel they should have children to complete their relationship. Many people have what we call a *maternal* or *paternal* urge – they want to have children, and it is a very important thing for them. When they can't have children, many look to doctors and medicine for help – even when it costs a lot of money, and the success rate is low.

The course lists specific types of **fertility treatment** that you have to know about. The exam could ask you about any of them – what they are, what benefits or problems there are, or what the religions think about them. Let's find out what they are. There are other forms of fertility treatment, but the

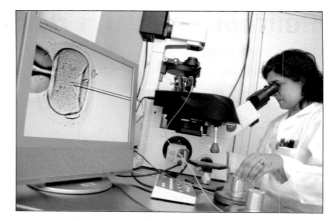

exam doesn't specify those, so you don't need to know them. Anything extra could impress the examiner, but it isn't needed.

IVF

IVF stands for *in vitro fertilisation*. *In vitro* means *in glass*. It makes the point that the egg and sperm are collected and brought together in a Petri dish. A number of these are done. They are kept warm for a few days, the sperm fertilise the eggs, and the eggs begin to develop. Now each egg has become about eight identical cells, and is called a blastocyst. Several of these are then placed into the woman's womb in the hope that a normal pregnancy will result.

IVF is used when the woman cannot conceive naturally. There is about a 25 per cent success rate. The egg and sperm could have come from the couple and/or donors. The egg and sperm will have been kept frozen ready for use and once fertilised any unused blastocysts must be destroyed within fourteen days by law.

Surrogacy

This is where another woman carries a pregnancy to full term for a couple. Conception is usually by one of the artificial methods on this page. It can be done using the couple's and/or donors' egg and sperm. The resultant child is then brought up as the child of the couple. It is used in cases where the woman can not medically carry a pregnancy. The surrogate will have agreed to bear the pregnancy. In the UK, although **surrogacy** occurs, it is illegal to pay someone to do it.

AID/H

AID/H is artificial insemination by donor/husband. Doctors collect several semen samples, which the man has produced by masturbating. The semen contains the sperm that are needed to fertilise the egg. The doctor uses a syringe to put the samples into the woman's womb when she ovulates, at a place which makes it more likely for fertilisation to happen. Hopefully, the egg will be fertilised. AIH is used when the husband has a low sperm count – the procedure is helping his sperm to fertilise his wife's egg. AID is used when he has no sperm count (he is infertile), or he has a genetic disease that he does not wish to pass on (this means his sperm are fertile, but the risk of passing on the disease is too great). The success rate of this treatment is very low.

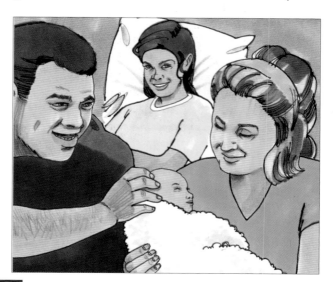

Now you have learned about fertility treatment

Religious attitudes to fertility treatment

You have already gained some idea of basic beliefs from pages 2–3. There are some more specific ones here to go with them.

Buddhist attitude

- Buddhists practise ahimsa – loving kindness and non-violence to all sentient beings.
- All lives are shaped by karma, and suffering in this life is from that karma.
- Life exists from conception.

Having families has never been a major focus of Buddhism. However, those who want but can't conceive children, suffer because of that. Buddhists see fertility treatment as showing compassion (loving kindness) to people in this situation. It is possible to see their predicament as a result of previous karma though – which they need to work through. There is concern over the throwing away of excess embryos, as this can be seen as killing.

Christian attitude

- Go forth and multiply (Genesis).
- God knows each of us intimately, and has set a plan for our life (Old Testament).
- Infertility is a call from God to adopt (Roman Catholic teaching).

There are a variety of Christian views. Some accept all fertility treatment as part of God's gift of medicine, and even an extension of Jesus' teachings of love. Roman Catholics however, see it as wrong, because children should be conceived by a couple within the confines of marriage. This is believed to be natural law. Many Christians hold a midway view. They accept fertility treatments, but see use of donor materials as adultery.

Hindu attitude ॐ

- The householder (grihastha) stage of life should lead to children in a family.
- All men come into the world burdened by ancestor debt. The only way to repay this is by fathering a son.
- Karma shapes our lifetimes, and we have to face difficulties to repay bad karma from the past.

Children are so important in Hinduism, especially boys. There is a pressure to have children, and if that means through artificial means, fine. Levirate marriage (conceiving a child with a second wife/husband) is accepted in Hinduism, so use of donor materials would be. Fertility treatment can also be seen as a compassionate way to help people, as is surrogacy.

Muslim attitude

- Allah gives life to whom he chooses (Qur'an).
- 'Marriage is my tradition' (Muhammad pbuh).
- Do not come near adultery or fornication for it is shameful (Qur'an).

Islam sees marriage and having children as a **duty**. There is the belief that Allah blesses couples with the gift of children, suggesting it is his will if someone is unable to have a child. Most Muslims will accept fertility treatments, though, seeing the knowledge as a gift from Allah. However, use of donor materials is seen as both adultery and fornication, so is considered wrong.

Jewish attitude

- Go forth and multiply (Genesis).
- Do not commit adultery (Exodus).
- There are several stories of women being 'helped' to conceive when obviously infertile in the Tenakh, such as 2 Kings 4:14–16.

Judaism accepts fertility treatment as long as no donor material is used. The egg and sperm must be from the couple. Use of donor sperm is considered to be adultery, which breaks one of the Ten Commandments. It also requires a man to 'waste seed' because the child will not be his – another rule broken. There is the concern over potential social problems for the child and parents when it learns how it came to exist.

Sikh attitude

- 'May you have seven sons' (a traditional wedding blessing).
- Any third person within a marriage is seen as adultery.
- God gives life, which is an expression of his will (Guru Granth Sahib).

Sikhism encourages couples to have children, and that is seen in the marriage blessing. For those Sikhs who cannot have children, any fertility treatment must not involve donor materials. This is considered to be a kind of adultery – one of the Four Abstinences. Although God chooses who will be born (which can mean accepting infertility as God's will), many Sikhs accept fertility treatment as God-given knowledge.

The Basics

1 Outline the attitude of one/two religions to each kind of fertility treatment.
2 Why do many religions **not** accept fertility treatment which uses donor materials?
3 **People should just accept being infertile as God's will.** Do you agree? Give reasons and explain your answer showing you have thought about more than one point of view.

Now you have learned about religious attitudes to fertility treatment

Helping others

The second portion of this topic is about how medical science tries to help people, and the religious attitudes to that.

All religions say that people should help each other. For some, looking after others is a duty from God – Christians, Muslims, Jews and Sikhs might say this. For others, it is helpful to their spiritual development to help others – Buddhists, Hindus and Sikhs might say this. Then again, it could be seen as an act of worship, or devoting yourself to God's work. So you'd expect religions to support medical science and its continued improvement. It isn't always the case, though, and there are areas of the newest medical advances that religious people are either concerned about or disagree with.

> **Think about these scenarios.**
> For each one, discuss with a partner whether you think the medical treatment is morally or ethically right: in other words, is it a good or bad thing in each case. The treatment to discuss is written in red.

Sam has been hit by a car. He needs an operation and many blood transfusions.

Caleb has very weak heart. He needs a transplant to save his life.

Jack's granddad has Parkinson's disease. Doctors say that stem cell therapy could help him to recover.

Jay and Shilpa's young son has a genetic disorder. They need tissue from a perfect match donor. Doctors have said they can genetically engineer the DNA of a new baby the couple could have, to provide the donor materials needed to help their son.

> *Do you still reach the same decision when the following extra information is available?*

- Sam's family do not believe it is right to have blood from someone else.
- Caleb's doctors have said the only available heart is that of a genetically modified pig.
- Stem cells come from embryos which are a few days old. The embryos are then discarded.
- Jay and Shilpa don't want another child – a new baby would be produced only to save the child they already have and want.

It is easy to make a decision on simple details, but when you learn more it becomes more difficult. Perhaps the most important thing is to know a little more about each of those medical treatments. You also need to know a little about cloning, experiments on humans, and **embryology**.

 Now you have thought about how medicine can help others

The medicine

The Human Embryo and Fertilisation Act (1990)

This covers three areas. Firstly, it regulates any fertility treatment that uses donated eggs or sperm, or embryos created through IVF. Secondly, it makes rules about the storage of eggs, sperm and embryos. Thirdly, it gives the guidelines and rules for any **experiments** on early stage human embryos. It was amended in 2000 and 2001 to allow the use of a dead man's sperm where it had been collected in his lifetime, and to allow doctors to create embryos to use in research on **therapeutic cloning**. These amendments were made for the purpose of improving medicine in the future, and the better understanding (and so tackling) of disease.

The whole point of this law was to set up rules for scientists to work within. It tries to show respect to embryonic life – by forcing embryos to be destroyed after fourteen days their development has been minimal. It also tries to show respect to people's lives by trying to find cures and ways to help people.

Embryo research

Embryo research is only allowed on embryos younger than fourteen days. Scientists try to learn more about the development of embryos, and also to learn more about disease, especially genetic diseases. The hope is that this research will help to find cures. It is impossible to study embryos when they are in the womb, so the only way is to use 'spare' embryos from fertility treatment or to create embryos just for research.

Stem cell research

Within embryos are stem cells. These are cells that can develop into any part of the human body – they have the ability to become anything. They are being used to 'grow' organs like kidneys, and also to help repair parts of the brain in sufferers of Parkinson's disease. Once the stem cells have been removed, the embryos die.

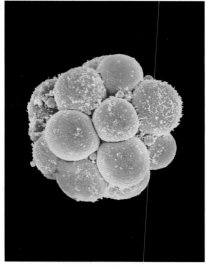

A human embryo less than fourteen days old.

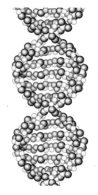

Genetic engineering

Everyone has DNA – it is what makes each of us unique. It contains all the reasons for why, who and what we are – it is like human programming. This programming is made up of 100,000 genes. Some of those genes are dangerous and even fatal – they make us susceptible to diseases, or even to being born with a disease. Scientists have worked on gene research and can modify the genetic make-up of cells to successfully treat hundreds of genetic disorders and diseases. This is called **human genetic engineering**.

Cloning

This is asexual reproduction – in other words creating a human foetus from one person, using an egg and cells. The foetus is an exact replica of the human it was cloned from. Dolly the sheep was the most famous example of cloning – it is illegal to clone humans.

Now you have learned about medical technologies

Thinking about the medicine

Task

In the exam, you could be asked why religious people agree or disagree with any of the medical technologies on the previous page.

Read the conversation between James and John below. They are discussing these technologies. Pick out their arguments to agree and disagree with each type of technology.

Copy and complete the table at the bottom of the page as you work through their conversation, using the information from the previous page as well.

James: Did you read about those scientists? They are cutting up embryos to do research on. That's experimenting on babies!

John: Yeah, but they can only do it up to fourteen days, so it's just a blob of cells really. And anyway, they are finding out stuff that will help people in the future.

James: It's still a baby, I think – well a 'going-to-be' baby. I think that is cruel and says their life isn't worth anything.

John: They have no nerves, so there is no pain. I think it is better to sacrifice them and learn, than to let babies be born with illnesses and stuff.

James: I bet you agree with stem cell research too then, don't you?

John: Certainly do. Those cells are like magic – they change into whatever you need them to be. Doctors will be able to grow organs, or help people with brain damage. The embryos are leftovers from IVF, so they would be destroyed anyway – I reckon it's a better use to take their stem cells out. Helps people that way.

James: It is still being disrespectful of life – even if it is only potential life. Life is supposed to be special and sacred. So what about cloning then?

John: Oh, I'm not sure about that. No sex, but there is a baby – doesn't seem right.

James: IVF is no sex, but a baby – and you agree with that.

John: Cloning is different. They don't even use two people to make the embryo. I think all babies should come from a mum and dad, not a mum and a bunch of her own cells! And what about the problems the clone could have? They have the same genetic age as the cells that made them – imagine being a baby with the genetics of a 50 year-old! You'd get all the ageing stuff way too early!

James: But it would mean you could design babies, like to provide a perfect match for someone who was ill with a disease. I think that is a good thing about it.

John: Well, in that case, you should accept genetic engineering. Scientists get the embryos and take out the DNA, fix it and put it back. That way the baby doesn't have the disease in the first place.

James: We are back to experimenting on embryos. I'm confused about what to think now!

Technology	What is it?	Benefits	Problems
Embryo research			

Now you have thought about the medical technologies and their ethics

Transplants and transfusions

Most people have absolutely no worries at all about this. They support both. In effect these procedures don't take life, don't mess with the living, and do help others. But, what are they?

Save a life
Give Blood

www.blood.co.uk

Transfusions

This is usually about blood and blood products (like plasma or platelets). If someone has to have an operation, they may need extra blood to replace the blood they lose during the operation. If someone has an accident and loses a lot of blood, they may need it to be replaced. This is what blood transfusions are all about. The blood that people are given must, in most cases match the blood they have – there are a number of different blood groups, and some are more common than others. Get the wrong blood and it could be fatal. Blood transfusions for humans have been happening since 1818, and blood types were only discovered in 1900 – so transfusion was a very risky procedure until then.

> There are always appeals for people to give blood. Why do you think blood services have to keep asking for more blood?

Transplantation

Organ transplantation happens because the organ in someone's body is failing, has failed, or is so damaged that it needs to be replaced. The first transplant procedure was done in 1905, and was corneal grafting (replacing part of the eye). The first organ transplant was done in 1954 – it took that long to get it right! Nowadays, organ transplanting is very common. Most organs are donated by the dead, who have carried a consent form, or whose families have agreed their bodies can be used to help others. Organs such as the heart, liver and kidneys are common transplant organs, but really most of the body can be used. Some people give up organs whilst still alive, for example, giving up one of their two kidneys, or donating a part of their liver. This is usually for a relative – so is an act of love – but there are cases in other countries where they sell the organ because they need the money. That is illegal in the UK. Recently, doctors have been able to genetically modify certain animals so that organs from their bodies can be used in humans – xenotransplantation.

> There are always appeals for people to carry donor cards. Why do you think the number of appeals increases all the time?

Task

1. Would you give blood? Explain your answer.
2. Would you carry a donor card? Explain your answer.
3. More people give blood than carry donor cards – why do you think that is?
4. Would you accept an organ from an animal if you needed one? Explain.
5. Do you think people should have to carry a card to NOT be a donor? This would mean that the body of anyone who dies could be used to help others. Explain your answer.

Now you have thought about transfusions and transplants

Religions and maintaining life

Don't forget to use the quotes on pages 2–3 and 7–8 to boost your knowledge here.

Buddhist attitude

- In many lifetimes, the Buddha gave up his own life to save that of others, for example, lying down before a starving lioness so that she could eat him and then feed her cubs.
- The Bodhisattva vow – to help all who need help.
- Cherish in your hearts boundless goodwill to all beings (Buddha).

In terms of transfusions and transplants, Buddhism leaves it to the individual's choice. It is a good thing in that you help others, usually selflessly. There are concerns about experimenting on embryos and on other technologies linked with embryos. One monk has said that until we know for sure the embryos feel no pain or have no consciousness of what is happening to them, we should not do experiments on them. However, it is the case that this work should help many people in the future, and so – in that sense – many Buddhists will cautiously accept the technologies.

Christian attitude ✝

- All life is sacred, and should be respected because it is given by God.
- Jesus helped others.
- Love one another (Jesus to his disciples).

Roman Catholics believe that any research using embryos is wrong and against natural law. A foetus should be given the same respect a person would have – and we wouldn't do this to people. Other Christians are similarly unhappy because they believe all life is sacred. However, many can see the potential benefit in the future to many people, and when the embryos used were to be discarded anyway, they see this as making something good from bad. Cloning is seen as playing God and therefore wrong.

Organ donation and blood transfusion are seen as acts of kindness. In fact, Pope Benedict XVI called it a 'free act of good will', and he himself has agreed to be a donor after his death. Most Christians agree with both, though Jehovah's Witnesses have now pioneered bloodless surgery because they disagree with having blood from someone else (the life is in the blood).

Hindu attitude

- Hinduism has stories where human body parts are used to help others.
- All things, including humans, are expressions of Brahman.
- Daya (compassion) and dana (charity) must be practised by Hindus.

There is nothing in the scriptures which prevents Hindus from being blood or organ donors. In fact, it fits well with their duties and efforts to attain moksa. It is up to the individual, though, to make the decision.

When it comes to things like cloning, that is not seen as creating souls (Hindus believe souls migrate into bodies) so is OK. Where embryo research uses live embryos, Hindus see this as wrong, because it is experimenting on human life.

Muslim attitude

- Whoever saves a life, it would be as if he had saved the life of all people (Qur'an).
- Shari'ah law prohibits the mutilation of a body.
- Do not take life – which Allah has made sacred – except for just cause (Qur'an).

Embryo research is wrong on live embryos. It is a life, which is sacred. If the tissue used in experiments is from a miscarried foetus or an abortion, then it would be acceptable to use it in research, which could benefit others. Cloning is playing God, and is therefore shirk (blasphemy).

There is a dilemma in Islam that we should not cut up dead bodies, but still have a duty to save life. **Transplant surgery** is seen as saving life, so Shari'ah law allows it as the lesser of two wrong things. Blood transfusion simply helps others, so is encouraged, even though it is not a common practice amongst Muslims in the UK.

Jewish attitude

- If one is in the position to be able to donate an organ to save another's life, it is obligatory to do so (Rabbi Moses Tendler).
- A basic principle of Jewish ethics is the infinite worth of a human being.
- It is forbidden to mutilate a body, and the whole body must be buried.

Genetic engineering is acceptable in Judaism if it is to get rid of disease, but not to improve G-d's creation (blasphemy). Research using live embryos is wrong. Embryos that are left over from IVF, for example, could be used, rather than creating embryos (sacred life) to experiment on.

Jews have an obligation to preserve human life. So, most rabbis would permit both transplants and transfusions. However, the time between certified death and removal of a heart is unclear, so heart transplants are not acceptable (the removal could have caused the death).

Sikh attitude

- Sewa – service to others as an act of worship.
- Life begins at conception, and is given by God.
- Caring for the sick has been part of Sikhism from the earliest days of the faith.

Sikhs do not agree with experiments on live embryos because life begins at conception. They would accept genetic engineering where it prevents disease, but not to improve or alter the body God has created. Cloning could either be helpful or against God – depending on the intention behind it.

Transplants and transfusions both help others. Service to others is a duty and whether by donating, or by being the surgeon who carries out the procedure, a Sikh does sewa. Since Sikhs believe that the body is just waste after death, it can be used to help others.

Many Sikhs believe that God gave humans this knowledge, so to not use the knowledge for the good of humans is wrong.

The Basics

1. Explain each of these terms – embryo research, genetic engineering, cloning, transplants, transfusions.
2. For each of them, explain the attitude of the religion(s) you have studied.
3. Why might a religious person disagree with any of them?

Now you know the religious attitudes

Humans and experiments

For the course, you have to think about whether it is right to experiment on humans, and what religions would say about that.

Scientists already do experiments on humans. They do observational tests, for example, to watch behaviour. They carry out surveys, and get people to keep logs of their feelings, emotions, temperature, pulse and so on. They interview people and collate the results. None of these cause any harm to people.

Scientists also test new drugs on humans. The humans usually volunteer, and are usually paid (in the UK) for being the guinea pigs. These drugs have already gone through years of checking and animal testing first, so it really is at the last point before public use – it is meant to be safe and useful when it gets to this stage. So again, there should be no harm to humans.

What we can see is that generally speaking, testing on humans is always meant to be safe. They are always carried out with the consent of the person.

Having said that, there are historical cases of testing having been done without consent, for example, the Nazis in the Second World War, the Japanese in China in the first half of the twentieth century. No one thinks that these tests were right. The people were victims of abuse. But what if people agree to the tests, and they go wrong? One famous example of this was in March 2006, when some volunteers had extreme reactions to the drugs they were testing. All recovered, but it was headline news.

INFORMED CONSENT TO EXPERIMENT

Principal investigators
Dr. R. J. Portman and
Dr. K. R. Singh

By signing below, I am indicating that I am at least 18 years of age, and I have read and understand the procedures described above. My questions have been answered to my satisfaction, and I agree to participate in this study.

Signed ....

Task

Your teacher will give each group one of the phrases below. Write on an A3 sheet. Take three minutes to write as many points as you can onto the sheet. Swap the sheet with another group. You then have four minutes to add extra points, and/or extend the points already on there in agreement or disagreement. Swap the sheet with a third group. You then have five minutes to read the comments, then add from your group or extend what is on there. Swap with a fourth group, and check the different ideas that have come out about the statement those groups have thought about.

If people agree to be guinea pigs, and if they are paid and they know what will happen, is it OK to test on them?

Why do scientists do experiments on humans?

Should there be limits and regulations to testing on humans?

Science needs answers for the future – people should be used as test subjects with or without their knowledge.

Why is testing on humans not as controversial as testing on embryos?

Testing on humans is like saying life isn't sacred or special.

More important – testing on people or embryos?

Now you have thought about testing on humans

Exam practice – revising this topic

You have probably seen these before in one form or another. They have many names depending on who has done them. We are going to call them 'thought maps'. They are brilliant to revise from and to – which might sound a bit weird, but let's explore them.

Look at the thought map. It has the topic idea in the centre, and it breaks up into the bits of topics that probably made up your different lessons. They then break up into the bits of information you got told in your lessons. The further from the centre, the smaller the detail – always the least easy to remember, but where the top marks get given in exams. So you could say you need to get to the outer limits in your revision. This one isn't complete – you need to do that, but you will have to put it on a bigger page with more space.

This one goes clockwise – so your brain can remember it more easily.

Thought maps are built up from the central topic to the far edge. Some people put all they know about each element of the central topic on the map, one element at a time; others add bits randomly. It is *your* thought map, so you make it to suit you.

Add the next layer of this thought map by adding examples, or extra points of information.

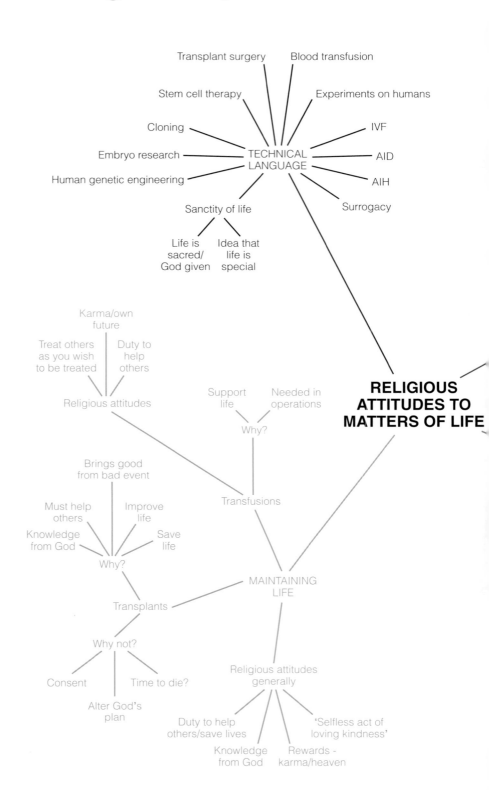

So, how does it act as a 'from and to' revision tool? Well, your teacher could give you a complete version, and you could look over it to see how much you are confident about. By highlighting the bits you know well, you end up with some bits which you need to do the serious revision on. You are working 'to' understanding it all.

At the end of the revision period, you can use it as a last minute checklist – so you'll be revising 'from' it.

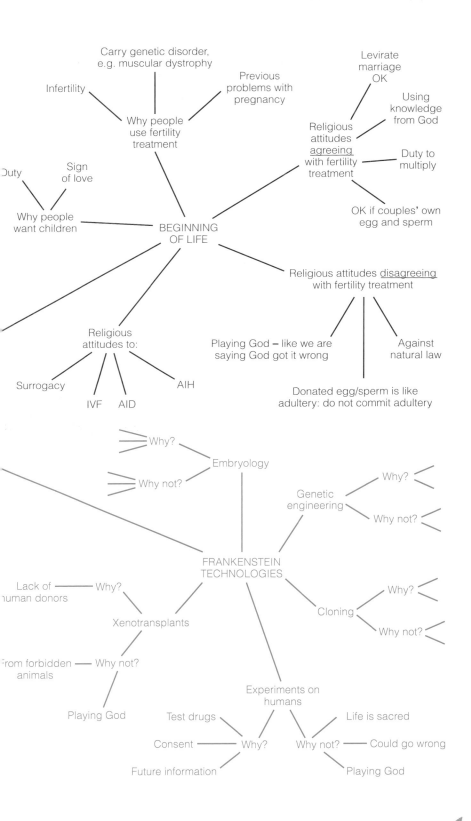

You might be more creative and be able to do extras on your thought map – if you can, draw (pictures do help most people remember). You just draw the image that makes the point. In writing, using different colours helps your mind get a fix on the different elements of the topic – your brain remembers the information in its colour grouping.

You can use these for any subject you want – if you like them, they will really improve your revision. When you have made them, stick them to walls at home, and look at them for short periods but often. In sight = in mind.

Now you know a revision technique

Topic Two Religious attitudes to the elderly and death

This topic is about the last part of life. It includes attitudes to the elderly, and the issues they face. It then goes on to look at attitudes to people at the end of their life, including **euthanasia**, life support and **hospices**. Finally, it is concerned with how religions view **life after death** – what they think will happen to us.

Two concepts key to the whole of this topic are **sanctity of life** and **quality of life**. You need to know what they mean.

Sanctity of life

This is the idea that all life is special. Many religions believe life is sacred because God created it (Christianity, Hinduism, Islam, Judaism, and Sikhism). Some religions believe life is special because it is the way we can achieve enlightenment (Buddhism and Hinduism). No one in the world believes that life is worth nothing. All the legal systems put murder as the worst **crime** you could commit, with the toughest **punishments**. Life is special, and deserves to be protected and cherished – not given up on. All religions believe that.

Quality of life

This is a description of how good someone's life is. It includes how comfortable they feel, how easy it is for them to live through each day, perhaps how much they have in terms of money and possessions. For this topic, it is about whether or not life is worth living because of the medical situation a person finds themselves in. Giving someone a good quality of life is part of the most basic teaching of all religions – that we should treat others as we wish to be treated.

> *Look at the scenarios on the right. In each case, is it about sanctity of life or quality of life? Or both? Explain your idea each time.*

- John is a serial killer. He murders people who are dying of terminal illnesses.
- Sarah visits her mother often to make sure she has everything she needs and is comfortable.
- Dave is very ill with cancer, and is constantly in a lot of pain. He is in a hospice.
- The local priest blesses those who are ill or dying, and visits them often.
- Pritti is a doctor in the Intensive Care Unit. She makes decisions about life support.

Now you have thought about the sanctity and quality of life

Getting old

Like it or not, most of us get old. We certainly all know old people – and by that we mean people beyond the age of **retirement**. Many of those people actually feel quite young, and would feel insulted to be classed as old. For this course, let's stick to 'those beyond the age of retirement', which means the over 65s – people who get a state pension and various other benefits because of their age. People who reach 75 get extra support. More and more people are living to be older – our life expectancy has increased a lot in the last century.

> *What issues are there for people who are beyond the age of retirement? With a partner check out these examples, and pick out the positives and the negatives.*

John: I fought in wars and won medals. In my lifetime I have seen many things and learned so much. I can pass on that knowledge and wisdom which comes from experience. I don't get much respect from people though – even after what I did for my country. Young people especially don't get it – they can be quite rude and ageist to me.

Susan: My health isn't as good as it used to be, and I need lots of medicines. My family are a big help to me, so that I can still live in my own home with their support and with visits from nurses regularly. I feel like I am the centre of my family – they all still come to me for a chat and advice. I've become what my Gran was – the matriarch!

Benjamin: I hated it when I had to retire. I worked for the government, so I had no choice. I suddenly had nothing to do with my day. I have got more used to it now, and I have lots of hobbies which I enjoy. Some of them are hobbies I had as a boy, and only now have the time (and money) to go back to them.

Brian: My pension isn't as good as my wages were, so I have less money than I used to. Sometimes money is very tight. I was very glad that the government gave us some extra heating money this year – I don't think I could have afforded to keep my home warm and eat and buy medicines if I hadn't got that.

Esther: I am very active even though I am eighty. I keep myself fit and healthy by walking and going to the OAP sessions at the local gym (they are free!). I don't think old people's voices are heard – we are just written off as a bit mad and out of touch. Some of us are but I think we are still worth listening to a lot of the time!

The Basics

1 What issues do you think old people face in Britain today?
2 Make a list of the good things about being old.
3 **Old people are no use to society**. What do you think? Explain your opinion.

Now you have thought about being old

Caring for the elderly

Our society cares for the elderly in a variety of ways. The exam could ask you about how we do that, so let's think – you already know this, so use your knowledge.

> *For each scenario below, work out whether there is any support and what that support is.*

Fred lives on his own, in his house. He has a state pension and his family visit him with extras every week.

Jane lives in sheltered accommodation. This means there is a warden who lives in another part of the building, and if she has a problem she can get his help quickly. A community room in the building means she gets to spend time with other people of her age. There is a doctor's surgery and a coffee room in the building as well. Her food is delivered by Meals on Wheels.

Nora lives in a **care home** for the elderly. She eats in the dining room with the others. Specially trained people work in the home, and provide all the care and support the people need. Her family visit when they can.

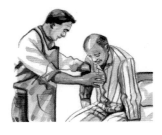

Andrew lives in his own house, but has carers to help him every day. One helps him get up and washed, and sorts out his breakfast. Later his pre-ordered meals will be delivered and another carer will come to prepare them for him. Finally the carer helps him to go to bed.

Religious attitudes to the elderly

Buddhism

- We may carry our mothers on one shoulder, and our fathers on the other, and look after them for a hundred years…we will still be in debt to them.
- Old people are a demonstration of anicca, so we learn from them.
- May all beings be happy (traditional Buddhist blessing).

Christianity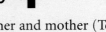

- Honour your father and mother (Ten Commandments).
- Listen to your father who gave you life and do not hate your mother when she is old (Proverbs).
- You shall rise up before the grey headed, and honour the aged (Leviticus).

Hinduism ॐ

- Whoever honours his father, honours the Creator himself. Whoever honours their mother, honours the earth itself (Mahabharata).
- The whole purpose of human existence is to benefit other people through one's life, possessions, thoughts and words (Bhagavata Purana).
- Let your mother be a god to you. Let your father be a god to you (Taittiriya Upanishad).

Judaism ♈

- Honour your father and mother (Ten Commandments).
- Do not cast me off in old age, when my strength fails me (Psalms).
- See that they [parents] eat and drink, and take them where they want to go (Talmud).

Islam ☪

- Your Lord orders that you…be kind to parents (Qur'an).
- May his nose be rubbed in the dirt who found his parents approaching old age [and he] did not look after them (Hadith).
- Your Lord has commanded that…you be kind to your parents. You should not even say 'Uff!' or criticise them…say 'Lord bless them, they nurtured, cherished and sustained me in childhood' (Qur'an).

Sikhism ☬

- It is the greatest sin to quarrel with parents who have given you birth and brought you up (Adi Granth).
- When a man acts in an unkind way towards his parents, his religious actions are worthless.
- Countless wrongs does the son, his mother forgives and remembers none (Guru Granth Sahib).

The Basics

1 It is quite obvious that all religions believe we should show respect to our parents. For each religion you are studying, explain how we can show respect to the elderly, and use quotations to say why.
2 In what ways do people support the elderly in our society?
3 Are there any forms of support that you think are unfair or wrong? Explain why.
4 **Religious people should care for their relatives as their first duty.** What do you think? Explain your opinion.

Now you have thought about caring for the elderly

Care for the dying

Everyone dies – we all know that. For some, death is sudden, or swift. For others, it comes at the end of a long and/or painful time. There is an argument about whether we should have the right to choose to die if we want to, and about how the dying should be cared for. For the exam, you need to be able to argue about both.

The hospice movement

Hospices are homes for the dying. People may go there until they die, or to give their families respite from looking after them for a while. On average people stay there for two weeks whether as a respite, or until death.

Originally, hospices were places for travellers, the sick and the needy to stay. They were set up by Christians. Over time, some of them began to specialise in looking after those who were dying.

When someone is dying, they can't be cured – only cared for. If that care covers all aspects of their being, they will not wish for euthanasia. This is the basic idea of hospices.

The aims of hospices:

1 To relieve the physical symptoms of illness. In other words, to get rid of as much pain as is possible. This includes things such as massage, meditation and relaxation. Often, medical treatment for the dying is very specialised – we call it palliative care.
2 To care for the emotional and spiritual well-being of the patient. Many dying people have unfinished business, which is a worry to them – the hospices help them to sort things out. Many patients are angry ('why me?') and hospices help them to come to terms with dying. Many patients need to be listened to, and given time – relatives often can't cope with this, but the hospices do.
3 To support the families of patients because they suffer too. Hospices provide many support networks and services for them, even after the death of the patient.
4 To educate others about caring for the dying, and to work out new, better ways to care for them – invaluable in the future, so that the experience built up in hospices can be used in other places.

Religious groups see hospices as the way forward for terminally ill people. God wants us to care for these people, to look after them, to express God's love for them; not to kill them.

Research Task

Find out about a hospice local to your school. Learn something of the work it does, the numbers of people it helps each year, whether it specialises in certain illnesses or age groups. Produce a report on that hospice for others in your class.

The national **charity** for hospices: www.helpthehospices.org.uk.
You can learn much about the hospice movement from their website.

St Ann's Hospice

This hospice was opened in 1971, and serves the Greater Manchester community. Its aim is to improve the quality of life of people with life-threatening illnesses. It aims to do this whilst supporting families and carers.

In a year, the hospice treats over 3000 patients, 42 per cent of whom return home after their stay. This costs almost £9 million, meaning that the hospice has to raise over £16,000 a day, which it does through voluntary contributions.

Cancer-related illness accounts for 95 per cent of patients. Each patient is given a personal care plan, which is tailored to meet their individual needs. This is what makes the support so unique and effective.

Supporting families

When someone is dying, there is a huge burden on their family. They have to try to support and care for their dying relative, but at the same time cope with their own feelings. Many people feel sad at the pain and loss, angry that this is happening, worried about the future, and they struggle to cope with everything.

Hospices try to support families, by having network support groups work through them. They will put families in contact with agencies who can help them.

How do religions support the families of the dying?

You have already read that the hospice movement was set up by Christians. Many hospices today retain those religious links – just check out a list of hospices on the internet or in a phone book and you will see how many are named after saints and other religious characters. Religions, of course, support the members of their communities who are dying, and also support their families.

Members of the religion can pray for the family and the dying. They can give comfort with readings from the holy book. They can be there to give emotional support, or just spend time with them. They can listen to them, and help them come to terms with what is happening. They can provide practical help to do things for the family – shopping and so on.

The Basics

1 Explain what a hospice is.
2 What are the aims of a hospice?
3 Describe the work of one hospice.
4 How do religions support the families of those who are dying?
5 **Hospices are the best way to help the dying.** What do you think? Explain your opinion.

 Now you have learned about hospices

Euthanasia

Euthanasia is mercy killing. It is helping someone to die, who is suffering from a terminal illness, or whose quality of life is less than they can bear, usually because of a degenerative disease. Euthanasia is done because of compassion – loving kindness.

The debates surrounding euthanasia have a long history! Hippocrates, a doctor from Ancient Greece, openly stated he would not prescribe drugs to help someone end their life. His stance has become the Hippocratic Oath, sworn by doctors in the UK, which says 'I will give no deadly medicine to anyone if asked, nor suggest such counsel…' In 1516CE, Thomas More defended euthanasia as the last treatment option for doctors to give, if the patient wanted it.

In the twentieth century, in most Western countries, groups exist to try to make euthanasia legal. In some countries, it is legal. The debate rages on.

Active euthanasia is when the dying person is killed to put them out of their suffering. What happens ends their life – their illness does not kill them.

Passive euthanasia is when the dying person is allowed to die through taking away the medical support they have – the illness is allowed to kill them.

Task

Look at these scenarios – which ones are active euthanasia and which ones passive?
1 Ben's doctor injects him with a medicine that stops his heart so that he dies.
2 Carl's doctor turns off his **life-support machine**.
3 Lisa decides to stop taking the medicine that is slowing down the growth of her brain tumour, so that it will kill her sooner.
4 Jean's husband puts a pillow over her face and suffocates her when her illness has become too painful to bear.

The law on euthanasia in the UK

Euthanasia is illegal in Britain. It can be seen as breaking the Suicide Act 1961, which forbids anyone from helping someone else to die and carries a fourteen year jail sentence. It can be also be viewed as manslaughter, or at worst, murder, which carries a life sentence.

Doctors do switch off life-support machines when patients have no sign of brain activity, and they do administer drugs to ease pain, which also shorten life. Neither of these is seen as euthanasia in the UK.

The Basics

1 What is meant by euthanasia?
2 Using examples, explain the difference between active and passive euthanasia.
3 Explain why doctors might feel unhappy about active euthanasia.
4 What is the law in the UK regarding euthanasia?
5 **Everyone should have the right to die if that is what they want.** Do you agree? Give reasons and explain your answer, showing you have thought about more than one point of view.
6 **Euthanasia is murder.** Do you agree? Give reasons and explain your answer, showing you have thought about more than one point of view.

Why euthanasia – or why not?

The exam often asks why religious people agree or disagree with euthanasia. Religious people are just the same as anyone else, and their reasons may be religious or secular. Work through the reasons on this page and decide which ones agree with euthanasia and which ones go against it.

No one has the right to take life – only God.

Everyone has the right to decide when they have had enough.

It is an act of kindness to help someone die if that is what they really want.

To allow euthanasia would encourage it – then people would force it for their own desires, for example, making a rich parent feel like a burden.

Euthanasia is another form of murder.

For some people, the only help we can give them is to help them die.

There can be miracle cures, and good can come out of terrible situations, so we should not seek euthanasia in case this is meant to be.

Can you add any other reasons why people agree or disagree with euthanasia?

The life-support issue

Doctors will switch off life-support machines. This is done with the consent of the family, and is always when the patient has no hope of recovery. Essentially, the machine is keeping the person alive by making their lungs breathe, monitoring their heart and feeding them intravenously.

Switching off the machine is not seen as euthanasia in the illegal sense, and doctors cannot be prosecuted. It is a recognition that medical treatment has failed – the patient is in effect already dead.

Not everyone agrees with switching off these machines. One famous example is that of Tony Bland. He was a Liverpool fan severely injured in the Hillsborough disaster (96 fans were crushed to death at an FA Cup semi-final in 1989). He suffered broken ribs, punctured lungs and severe brain damage. He was on a life-support machine until 1993 when the courts granted his parents' wish to have his treatment ended so that he could die.

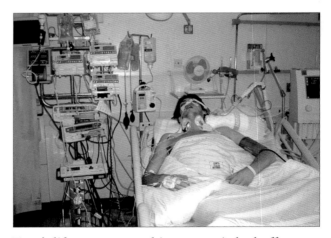

Tony's life-support machine was switched off on 22 February, and he died on 3 March.

Life and SPUC both disagreed and mounted campaigns to stop the life-support machine being switched off. They claimed that it is not our place to end life, but to protect and save it.

The Basics

1. Explain why some people agree with euthanasia as an option.
2. Explain why some people disagree with euthanasia.
3. Explain different attitudes to life support.

Religious attitudes to death and euthanasia

Buddhist attitude

Buddhists believe all life is special. It deserves protection. Death is inevitable – just part of the journey. It is wrong to speed up that death though, because everyone has karma to work through, and the suffering leading up to death may be part of that karma.

- I will abstain from taking life (the First Precept).

- At the hour of death, a king and a beggar are equal because no amount of **wealth** or relatives can affect or prevent death (Lama Zopa Rinpoche).

- A primary guiding principle in Buddhism is the relief of suffering.

- 'In the event a person is definitely going to die…is either in great pain or has virtually become a vegetable, and prolonging his existence is only going to cause…suffering for others, the termination of his life may be permitted according to Mahayana Buddhist ethics (Dalai Lama).

Many Buddhists would not support euthanasia – life should be protected and suffering is part of our karma. However, it is important to make death as comfortable as possible, so Buddhism supports the hospice movement which helps people to have a 'good' death. Our state of mind is important when we die because it is a key to shaping our next lifetime. If we are angry, anxious and upset, then this will have a negative impact. If we face death with acceptance, then the rebirth is better. Having said that, the intention of every act is key – and euthanasia is usually done out of compassion, and with the wishes of the person who dies, so is a 'good' death.

Christian attitude

Life is sacred because it is created by God. We should protect life as much as possible. Generally, although Christians talk about being with God after death, there is no wish to hasten death. The hospice movement is seen as the compassionate and proper way to help those who are dying whilst they wait for God to take their life.

- God created life in his own image (Genesis).

- You shall not kill (Ten Commandments).

- I, your God, give life, and I take it away (Old Testament).

- It is the teaching of the Catholic Church that life be respected from conception until natural death.

- Doctors do not have an overriding obligation to prolong life by all available means (Church of England).

Attitudes to euthanasia are diverse in Christianity but most Christians do not agree with it. It is seen by many, such as the Roman Catholic Church, as a failure of the systems available – and even as murder. The Church of England accepts passive euthanasia, where nothing can be done for the patient but does not agree with active euthanasia. The Dutch Protestant Church believes that the patient can lose all quality of life, and that God would not wish for their suffering to continue. These Christians accept active euthanasia, and even bless people before the procedure is done.

For some questions on religious attitudes, see pages 27–28

Hindu attitude 🕉

Hindus believe that our atman (soul) lives through many lifetimes, and that each life is shaped by the words, actions and thoughts of the previous ones. This means that any suffering in this life is intended so that bad karma from previous lifetimes can be worked through. Cutting short this life by euthanasia just puts off that task – so is generally seen as wrong.

- Ahimsa (non-harming) is a basic principle of Hinduism.
- Compassion (loving kindness) and respect (including for all life) are other key principles of Hinduism.
- The result of a virtuous action is pure joy; actions done from emotion bring pain and suffering (Baghavad Gita).
- The one who tries to escape from the trials of this life by taking their own life will suffer even more in the next life (Yajur Veda).

There is great respect for age and the wisdom associated with it in Hinduism. This protects many older people from even the suggestion of euthanasia, but it does not mean that some of them will not choose to die rather than be a burden on their family (as they see it). It would be accepted that they refuse food or medicines, but it would be wrong for them to be euthanised. Active euthanasia can be seen as trying to escape problems, so it is wrong for the person to seek euthanasia. Also, if the person trying to help them die is doing so because they can't cope with their own feelings, then that is wrong. Hindu principles are to look after, care for and support the dying until their natural death.

Muslim attitude

In Islam, any form of self-harm or self-killing is wrong. Basically, it is the decision of Allah when a person should die, which means any interference into what is Allah's plan is wrong.

- Neither kill nor destroy yourself (Qur'an).
- No one can die except by Allah's leave, that is a decree with a fixed term (Qur'an).
- Whoever kills a man…it shall be as if he had killed all mankind (Qur'an).
- Do not take life – which Allah has made sacred – except for a just cause (Qur'an).
- Euthanasia is zulm – a wrong doing against Allah (Shari'ah law).

The Muslim attitude to euthanasia is very straightforward. Life is sacred, made by Allah. It will be ended when Allah decides – not when the person themselves or their family or a doctor decides. There is a story of a man who was helped to die because of the great suffering he was in. The man and his 'helper' were both denied paradise as a result. No one knows the plans of Allah. This is called al-Qadr or the predestination of Allah's will. In other words, Allah has planned for this experience and it must be important. So no one should make that decision to end life – it will happen when Allah wills it. This does not mean that a person couldn't refuse the medicine which is keeping them alive longer. In many cases, passive euthanasia would be accepted – where there is absolutely no hope.

The Basics

Using pages 26–29, read through the religion(s) you have studied and answer the following questions:

1 Use teachings to explain their attitude to life.
2 Use teachings to explain their attitude to when we die.
3 Use teachings to explain whether or not they agree with euthanasia.
4 Describe their beliefs about life after death.

See page 28 for more questions.

Jewish attitude

In Judaism, life is sacred. Death should be a calm experience where possible. Attitudes to euthanasia vary – but are mainly focused on the type of euthanasia. The experience of the mass murder of the Holocaust also influences attitudes to unnatural death.

- You shall not kill (Exodus).
- G-d gives life, and G-d takes away life (Psalms).
- For everything there is a reason, and a time for every matter under heaven: a time to be born, and a time to die; a time to plant and a time to pluck up what has been planted (Ecclesiastes).
- If there is anything which causes a hindrance to the departure of the soul then it is permissible to remove it (Rabbi Moses Isserles).
- One who is in a dying condition is regarded as a living person in all respects (Talmud).

For Judaism, the question is whether euthanasia shortens life or shortens the act of dying. The latter would be acceptable, so that the person can have a 'good death'. Life and death belong to G-d, though G-d would not want to see us suffer. It is important to protect and support life, to care for the dying, but it is wrong to end their life through active euthanasia, because that is G-d's role. In the Holocaust, millions of Jews were murdered as Hitler attempted to wipe out the entire population of the Jews in Europe. This makes it even more important to safeguard and respect life, and euthanasia can at times be seen as throwing that life away.

Sikh attitude

Life is sacred, and all souls are on journey through many lifetimes, according to Sikhism. Liberation from rebirth is the eventual goal, but each life has been shaped by the words and actions of previous ones. As a result, suffering is part of the karma being worked through from a previous lifetime.

- God sends us and we take birth. God calls us back and we die (Guru Granth Sahib).
- A sign of divine worship is the service (sewa) of others (Adi Granth).
- The sign of a good person is that they always seek the welfare of others.
- Sikh gurus set up **hospitals** and medical treatment for Sikhs – this has continued to the modern day.
- All life is sacred and should be respected (Guru Granth Sahib).

There is no place for mercy killing in Sikhism. The Sikh gurus set up hospitals and treatment centres for the sick and dying. Many Sikhs work within the health service, which they see as sewa – service to others. Active euthanasia, then, would be considered wrong. The suffering involved in terminal illnesses is from the karma of previous lifetimes, and has to be worked through. A Sikh's role in these cases is to care for the dying, rather than speeding up their death. That care is the respect that their sacred life deserves until God decides they should die.

Task

With a partner, come up with as many reasons to agree and disagree with these statements as you can.

Euthanasia should be available to anyone who wants it.

Religious people should never accept euthanasia.

For some more questions on religious attitudes, see page 27.

Life after death in six religions

Buddhism

Buddhists believe in rebirth. There is no permanent soul, rather a mix of ever-changing skandhas – emotions, feelings, intelligence and so on. After the death of the body, this mix fuses with an egg and sperm at conception. The thoughts, actions and intentions of each life shape the quality of the next. The goal is to achieve enlightenment, and stop being reborn.

Christianity ✝

Christians believe in the physical resurrection of the body. At death, the body waits until Judgement Day. Catholics call this Purgatory. At judgement, each person will face God and Jesus to evaluate their deeds. If they were good in life, they will go to heaven, which is paradise and wonderful forever. If they were bad, they will go to hell for eternal punishment.

Hinduism

Hindus believe in reincarnation. Their atman (soul) lives through many lifetimes, each one shaped by the thoughts, words and actions of their past lifetime(s). Its goal is to achieve enlightenment and become one with the Ultimate Reality and stop being reincarnated.

Islam

Muslims believe in resurrection. At death, the body waits in the grave (barzakh) and sees the events of its life. This can be quick or very slow and painful. On Judgement Day, people are sorted according to their beliefs and actions. The wicked are cast into hell; the truly good go straight to Paradise. All others cross Assirat bridge, carrying the book of their deeds (sins make it heavier). The bridge is sharp, and so they are purified from sin before going to Paradise.

Judaism

Judaism focuses on this life, rather than the next. Some teachings mention a heavenly place. Jews talk of the 'world to come', which is when the Messiah will come to rule the earth in peace. That is life after death because the dead will be woken to live through that time.

Sikhism

Sikhs believe in reincarnation. The soul is born into many lifetimes, whose quality is decided by the words, thoughts and deeds of the previous lifetime(s). The point of each life is to serve and worship God, so that eventually the soul can be reunited with God (Waheguru) and stop being reincarnated.

Last thoughts about the end of days

The exam could ask you what we mean by *death*, and it is a difficult term to explain without using the word 'dead'. Also, there is some debate about it, and it is part of the reason why switching off a life-support machine is so contentious.

> Whose right is it to choose death?

What is death?

So, is it – when your heart stops?

> Pick out the reasons below that say why people should be able to choose what happens with their life, and those that don't. Can you think of any more?

There is definitely no heartbeat in a dead person! However, there is an illness where a person's heart stops then restarts. Also we see on hospital programmes on TV that there is a procedure to restart a heart when it stops. Finally, for some operations the heart has to be stopped at a certain point. In all these cases the person keeps living.

> My life belongs to God. I don't have the right to decide when I die.

Is it when we stop breathing?

Dead people don't breathe. However, people can hold their breath. Other people need ventilators to breathe. We don't say those people are dead.

> Letting one person choose death opens the door to people forcing relatives to choose death too.

Is it when our organs pack up?

If none of our organs worked, we would not be alive. However, thousands of people live with damaged or not working organ(s).

> If I can refuse medical treatment, I should be able to ask for help to die.

Is it when our brain stops functioning?

Doctors check the brain stem for electrical activity when a decision about life support is being made. Once the brain stem has stopped working, you can't recover from whatever problems you have. Machines could keep your body alive, but you won't ever regain consciousness, or be able to function.

> I decide on everything else in my life, so why not death as well.

So, we could say that no heartbeat, no breathing, no organs working and no brain stem activity are all characteristics of a dead person. The point of death, though, seems to be when the brain is no longer able to send instructions to the rest of the body to do all the things it needs to do.

Many people believe we should have the right to decide when we die – if only in the case of a painful and terminal illness. This is called *self-determination*. Check out the website of the Voluntary Euthanasia Society – www.ves.org.uk – for a look at this argument.

> My body, my life – should be my right to die.

Exam practice – revising the details

These are revision styles that worked for these young people. Perhaps they will work for you.

Our teacher pointed out that religions have a set of fundamental ideas. So I learned those key ideas, and applied them every time to my questions. It didn't give me full marks for a question – I had to learn some specifics for that! It did give me a really good start, which got me over half marks every time. So Christians think life is sacred – that applies to being born, dying, using drugs, treatment of prisoners, helping the poor – the list goes on and on (but my revision didn't need to!).

Emma

I made a set of flashcards, and got someone to test my knowledge regularly using them. Put images and words onto some cards, such as words to define, or religious ideas to link to death. Then someone shows one, and you talk about it. I even got my mum to help – so she knew I was revising!

Jack

Pictures help me, and pictures with labels rather than just words work even better for me. Get pictures of as many of the things you study as you can. Then you can think of the image in the exam, and it will help you remember. For example, a picture of someone dying with the options and the attitudes around them.

Carlton

When we did tests, before she marked them, our teacher went through each question telling us what we should have put. She told us the range of answers (well, she asked us to tell her as a class actually), and also what an examiner would be looking for in an answer. We had to guess at our mark and grade for the test. It really sharpened up my understanding of how to answer questions and made me read my answers properly – I never did that when I got tests back. This all helped me learn from my mistakes and improve my exam performance.

Ronnie

When my teacher taught us to do thought maps, I just got it all really quickly. See Topic 1 pages 16–17. Making them helped me revise. Looking at them helped me revise. Checking before the exam gave me confidence I had revised well. I used colours and loads of little pictures. Then, in the exam, I could picture each thought map in my head – it helped a lot. I liked them so much I did them for every subject.

Samira

Improving your exam performance

We are going to look at a couple of techniques for improving marks – these don't rely on what you have learned. They are about *how* you tackle the exam questions.

Checking the paper

I know, all the teachers tell you millions of times *read the paper before you start*. Most people don't follow that advice. Those who do, often just skim through it without really taking any notice of it. So, why bother checking?

Do you panic before or in exams? Many do, and it affects their performance. How many times have you done a test, and afterwards swapped answers with friends. Then you realise you put the wrong thing for some questions – but you knew the right answer – doh!

Reading through the paper first can act as a calming exercise, reducing that panic/stress level. Make it part of your exam habit.

Another thing – take a highlighter into the exam. As you read the paper, highlight the key words in the questions. There are two sorts of key words – command words, which tell you what to do, such as *Explain* and *Why*. Get those wrong and kiss goodbye to decent, or even any, marks. Then there are trigger words, which are the subject of the question. If the question is about reasons *for* euthanasia, don't write about reasons *against* it – you won't get any marks.

Checking your answers

When you have finished answering all the questions in an exam, what do you do?

Teachers say: 'smart people check their answers'. Do you?

You do? Excellent. BUT, *how* do you check your answers?

Most people read the question again, then read their answer again. They think it is fine, then move on to the next question. They don't spot many changes or additions needed.

Here is a better way…

Our brains are lazy, and will just limit our ideas if we can read an answer. They take the route already followed and so usually don't see a different idea. Using this technique your brain has to do some work. This way, your brain might give you some more marks through new things to say.

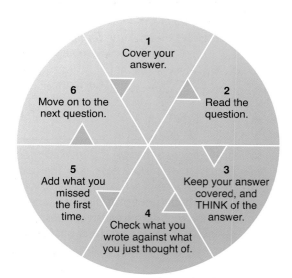

1 Cover your answer.

2 Read the question.

3 Keep your answer covered, and THINK of the answer.

4 Check what you wrote against what you just thought of.

5 Add what you missed the first time.

6 Move on to the next question.

When asked to list drugs, people often list **illegal drugs** – heroin, cocaine, marijuana and so on. They tend to forget those drugs that we meet on a daily basis – alcohol, **caffeine** and tobacco.

You will find out later that it is actually the use of alcohol and tobacco, legal drugs, that cause the most deaths, crime and violence of any drugs in our society.

> Only a complete fool would take drugs!

> Some drugs are OK if you don't overdo it.

> Everybody uses drugs.

> *Why do you think this is the case?*

> *Discuss the views of the young people above. What reasons can you think of to agree and disagree with each of them?*

So – what is a drug?

Simply put, a drug is any substance that, if consumed, will affect the way our bodies and mind work. They can be divided into four categories depending on the effects they have. There are stimulants, depressants, hallucinogens and opioid analgesics.

Stimulants (uppers) work by acting on the central nervous system to increase the activity of the brain. Depressants (downers) do exactly the opposite; they also work on the central nervous system, but they slow down the brain activity. Hallucinogens act on the mind, distorting vision and hearing. Opioid analgesics have a painkilling effect.

> *Make a list of drugs you know the names of. Can you categorise each by one of those four terms?*

For this unit, you have to be aware of the range of drugs used legally and illegally in society. You need to understand the different reasons people have for using drugs and the effects that drug use has on them and society in general. You need to be aware of the debate about the **classification** and legal status of some drugs. You will look at the problems **drug abuse** causes and evaluate the effectiveness of methods aimed at reducing drug taking.

You need to learn to put this knowledge into a religious perspective. To do this you must understand some religious teachings about the body and mind. You need to apply these teachings to the issues so that you can effectively explain religious attitudes, for example, to the use of social and **recreational drugs**. What is the response of religious believers to drug users?

A good place to start is to think about the religious teaching of the *sanctity of life*.

> *If someone believes all life is a gift from God, valuable, holy and having a purpose, what do you think they will say about drug use? Will they say all drugs are wrong? Will the teachings affect the rules that religious people live by? If so, how?*

Cocaine Heroin GAS CANNABIS Crack Coffee LSD Alcohol Anabolic steroids Aspirin Tobacco Ecstasy Magic mushrooms Skunk Aerosols Paracetamol Morphine POPPERS Amphetamines Antibiotics

Now you have begun to think about drugs

33

Drug use

The reasons people take drugs are almost as varied as the drugs that are available. Most people, at some point during their life, will use drugs for medical reasons. Drugs prescribed by a doctor, or bought over the counter at a chemist, are intended for a good purpose – to make us well. No one is going to reasonably say that this is wrong, and all religious traditions support the use of medically prescribed drugs. This unit is concerned with the reasons people take legal and illegal drugs for non-medical use.

Legal drugs, such as alcohol, caffeine and tobacco, are part of our social life. Just look at how many coffee bars, pubs and clubs there are in towns and cities – this shows that these drugs are simply part of our society. However, the recent ban on smoking in public places is recognition of the dangers that nicotine use poses to users (smokers) and non-users (passive smoking).

The dangers posed by some drugs are such that the government has deemed it necessary to make their sale and use illegal through the Misuse of Drugs Act, 1971. Drugs such as heroin, cocaine, amphetamines and cannabis pose serious threats to the users and society in general. Consequently, far fewer people use illegal drugs because they not only have health risks, but are against the law.

	Strongly agree	Agree	No opinion	Disagree	Strongly disagree
Anyone caught experimenting with illegal drugs should be expelled from school/college.					
You need alcohol to make a social occasion go well.					
Smokers should have to pay their own health care bills.					
Cannabis should be legal.					
Alcoholics are a drain on the country financially and in social terms.					
Glue sniffing is harmless adolescent fun.					
People should take medication only when they desperately need it.					
Society has a duty to help heroin users give up heroin.					
People who work with young people have a duty to be a positive role model when it comes to drugs.					
The drug you take depends on your cultural and social background.					
Children under fourteen should not be allowed to drink caffeine-based drinks.					
The government should make smoking and chewing tobacco products illegal.					
If people stopped smoking and drinking, the government would lose millions.					
What you do in the privacy of your own home should be your business and no one else's, as long as no one is hurt.					

Task

Complete the questionnaire, saying how much you agree or disagree with each statement. Discuss your answers in class. Try to come up with three reasons to agree and disagree with each.

Why use drugs?

Ask ten people why they first took a drug and you will probably get ten different answers. The same could be said of twenty people. If your parents drink or smoke, ask them why they continue – they will probably give you the same reasons as anyone who takes drugs. What about you? Do you use any drugs? Have you ever stopped to think about why you do, is it your choice or are you simply giving in to the pressures and temptations around you?

Task

Make a list of reasons why people use drugs. You may be asked exactly that question in the exam. Are there different reasons for using different types of drugs? Try to give some examples of drugs taken for specific reasons.

I like the risk

REBELLION

Boredom

It's fun

My friends do it

Easy to get them

CURIOUS

Can't give it up

Makes me feel grown up

Escape

There's no real harm

Enjoy it

So, someone whose life is tough, and has lots of personal problems, may turn to drugs. But not everyone does – why not? Some people seem to have everything and yet they turn to drugs – why? Some people just enjoy the habit. Clearly, drug use is very much a personal issue.

The reasons that drugs are used can be classified into broad areas:

- *Experimental* – to see what it's like.
- *Recreational* – some drugs are used in a social setting.
- *Experiential* – some drugs are used because of their effects, for example, they make us feel better or calm us down.
- *Addiction* – some drug takers become addicted and cannot stop themselves using the drug, their bodies cease to function properly without it, so giving it up often needs specialised help.

The Basics

1 What is a drug?
2 What are legal drugs? Give examples.
3 What are illegal drugs? Give examples.
4 Make a list of reasons why some people use drugs. Remember to explain the reasons fully.
5 **Taking drugs is a personal choice – it should have nothing to do with anyone else.** Do you agree? Give reasons and explain your answer.

> *Can you fit any drug into any of these areas?*
> *Or does it depend on the drug?*
> *We'll come back to this later in the topic.*

 Now you have begun to think about why people take drugs

Tobacco

Tobacco Fact File

- About 13 million adults in the UK smoke – 29 per cent of all males and 25 per cent of all females.
- 80 per cent of smokers started as teenagers.
- It is now illegal to sell tobacco products to anyone under the age of 18.
- About 25 per cent of 15-year-olds smoke, even though it is against the law to sell them tobacco.
- 120,000 people die every year from smoking-related illness – that's 330 a day.
- Smoking causes 30 per cent of all cancer deaths.

- One in two smokers will die because of their habit.
- More than 17,000 children under 5 are treated in hospital every year because of passive smoking.
- Over 4000 different chemicals can get into your bloodstream because of smoking; these include DDT, tar, nicotine, arsenic, phenol, ammonia, naphthalene and cadmium.
- Smoking inside public places has now been made illegal in many European countries, including all parts of the UK.

> *Why do people smoke?*
> *Are the reasons different to those for taking illegal drugs?*
> *Why is it more acceptable to smoke than use other drugs?*
> *Do you think smokers understand the risks?*

Kicking the habit

The government has invested large sums of money in raising awareness about the damaging effects of smoking. Tobacco products are taxed heavily and some of this money is used to fund NHS quitting programmes. But why should people give up?

Cost – If you smoke, work out how many you smoke a day. How many packs a week is that? Multiply by 52 for the weeks in the year. Now multiply by £5 which is about the average price for a packet of cigarettes. That is one year's cost to you. What else could you spend that money on?

Health – Yours and the people around you. Smoking is one of the most dangerous things anyone can do to damage themselves. But smoking is also very harmful to others because of the effects of passive smoking. Millions of pounds are spent in the NHS dealing with smoking-related illness. Just think how much could be done with that money if no one smoked.

Environment – Smoking pollutes the environment. This was known as early as the seventeenth century when James I famously banned smoking in court because of its disgusting odour. Think of the litter that smoking produces and the trees cut down to make the cigarettes and their packets in the first place.

Smoking – the effects

> *So what does smoking do to you?*

Short term

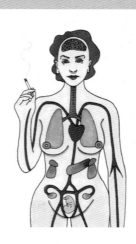

- You smell
- Stains fingers and teeth
- Causes bad breath
- Dries the skin
- Causes wrinkles
- Affects sporting performance

Long term

- Coronary heart disease
- Emphysema – affects breathing/lungs
- Cancer of the mouth, throat, lungs, bladder
- Pregnant women who smoke risk the health of their baby

Share and share alike!

Smoking doesn't only affect smokers.

Think about three main factors for giving up. How might it benefit others if someone stops smoking?

Passive smoking

Anyone in a smoking environment will be subjected to passive smoking. They will breathe in the fumes of the cigarette tip whilst it is burning and also the fumes that are exhaled by the smoker.

It does the same to everyone – it can irritate the eyes, nose and throat. It leads to headaches and nausea. It increases breathing problems for asthmatics and increases the number and severity of the attacks they suffer.

Smoking can have a greater effect on children because they are still growing. It can also affect the normal growth of their lungs. For adults it increases the chances of developing heart disease and a number of cancers.

Make a list of the potential dangers of smoking in the home.

When a pregnant woman smokes the unborn baby smokes too. Anything the mother takes in passes through the umbilical cord and into the baby. Babies born to pregnant women often show symptoms of the effects of smoking. They can be premature and underdeveloped. They are more likely to suffer respiratory illnesses as their immune systems have been affected by the mother smoking.

Much of Europe has now introduced no smoking policies in all public buildings. The smoking ban has been implemented throughout the whole of the UK. When it was introduced many people complained that it was against civil liberties and people should have a right to smoke if they chose.

NO SMOKING.
It is against the law to smoke in these premises

What do you think? Is it a good idea to prevent people smoking in public buildings? Would you extend the law to include all public places, even outside? Why do you think some pubs, clubs and restaurants objected to the ban?

Organisation Profile

Action on Smoking and Health (ASH) is a campaigning, public health charity that works to eliminate the harm caused by tobacco. It challenges the tobacco industry, which it feels is not honest about the effects of tobacco. Obviously, the future of tobacco companies relies on people being smokers. It is their business to increase the number of smokers, not decrease them. Check out ASH and the truth about tobacco at www.ash.org.uk.

ash.
action on smoking and health

The Basics

1. Why do some people smoke?
2. Explain some of the health risks of smoking.
3. Give three reasons why you think it is hard for smokers to quit.
4. How do you think the taxes raised from cigarette sales should be used?
5. What is passive smoking?
6. **Religious people who smoke are doing nothing wrong.** What do you think? Explain your opinion

Alcohol

Alcohol Fact File

- One in eleven children in the UK live in a family with alcohol problems.
- Alcohol misuse costs the NHS up to £1.7 billion every year.
- The average alcohol consumption of 11–13 year olds is 10.1 units of alcohol a week.
- Deaths from alcohol-related diseases in the UK are increasing year on year.
- Nearly half of all household fires are linked with someone who has been drinking.
- In the UK, eleven people are killed by drunk drivers every week, many more are seriously injured.
- Over 100,000 drivers every year test positive for alcohol.
- Heavy drinkers/smokers are 150 times more likely to get cancer of the throat/mouth.
- Half of all adult head injury patients are drunk when admitted to hospital.
- Drunkenness is a factor in the cause of many violent crimes, including GBH and rape.
- Many teenage mums admit they were drunk when they became pregnant.

Most adults have tasted alcohol and over 70 per cent of adults in the UK enjoy a drink at least once a week. More and more young people have tasted alcohol, and it is part of growing up as far as some people are concerned. The law states that it is illegal to sell or buy alcohol for anyone under the age of 18. The only exception is in licensed premises where 16- and 17-year olds can have a drink with a meal. Even those over 18 can't just drink what they want, where they want. Many cities and towns have alcohol-free zones to prevent people drinking on the streets. The heavy **fines** retailers can incur mean that increasingly shops are refusing to sell alcohol and tobacco to under 21s and insist on ID being shown by anyone they think may be under this age.

> *What do these facts tell you about the dangers of alcohol misuse?*

> *Why do you think these regulations exist?*

The Basics

(Use this double page to help you answer these questions)

1 List some of the reasons why people drink.
2 What are the short-term effects of alcohol use?
3 How does alcohol misuse affect:
   i. the drinker
   ii. their family
   iii. society in general.
4 **Religious people should never drink alcohol.** What do you think? Explain your opinion.
5 Check out the website http://www.drinkaware.co.uk/home.

Discussion point

The government collects taxes from the sale of legal drugs. What do you think should happen to this money? Why do you think legal drugs are taxed so highly?

Alcohol – the effects

Alcohol affects people in different ways. Things like your size and weight, what you drink and how much, whether you have eaten and the mood you are in when you drink, can all influence the effects you feel from alcohol. After just a couple of drinks most people will become more relaxed and talkative, which is why many people think it is a stimulant. In fact, alcohol is a depressant. It slows down your system and reflexes, which is why many people have accidents when they are drunk.

The long-term effects

You can have a great time when drinking, which is why many people do it. However, like most things it needs to be in moderation to ensure that there is not a heavy price to pay. Alcohol abuse can have a very damaging effect on the drinker, their family and society. This is why many religious traditions do not agree with drinking alcohol.

Regular alcohol abuse can have serious physical and psychological effects. These include:

- Decrease in brain tissue and function
- Impotence and infertility
- Heart disease and failure
- Liver disease and failure
- Anxiety and depression
- Obesity – alcohol has a high calorific value
- Skin reddening and poor circulation

The short-term effects of alcohol

- Increased aggression
- Loss of control and judgement
- Inability to work
- Addiction and dependency

What sort of risks might someone take when their judgement is impaired?

Clearly these effects can be very damaging to anyone who becomes an alcoholic. But what about their families? How might they suffer? And what about society in general? Does alcohol misuse affect others?

A quick glance at caffeine

Caffeine is a stimulant found in tea, coffee and many soft drinks and energy drinks. It is a stimulant often used to ward off drowsiness and increase alertness. Most people enjoy caffeine drinks and never think of them as a drug. However, too much caffeine can cause restlessness, insomnia, upset stomach and excitability. It is possible to become addicted to caffeine and suffer the 'caffeine jitters'.

Organisation Profile

Alcohol Concern is the national agency on alcohol misuse. They work to reduce the incidence and costs of alcohol-related harm and to increase the range and quality of services available to people with alcohol-related problems and their families.

 Alcohol Concern
Making Sense of Alcohol

Task

Design an advert to warn people about the dangers of caffeine

Now you have begun to think about alcohol

Let's talk drugs

Coke – Charlie – snow – c – base   *rock – wash – stone*   *E – Mitsubishis – Rolexes – dolphins – MDMA*

This is only a quick look at drugs. Check out websites such as www.lifebytes.gov.uk and www.release.org.uk to find out more. Local police forces and **young offenders'** teams are usually happy to come into school and give talks about drugs too.

Drug classification

The law regarding illegal drugs comes under the Misuse of Drugs Act, 1971. It lists three classes of drugs, and gives penalties for possession (having the drug for personal use) and supplying (having more than is needed for personal use, therefore intending to sell it).

Class A drugs: For example, cocaine, crack, ecstasy, heroin. Up to seven years' **imprisonment**/fine for possession; up to life imprisonment/fine for supplying.

Class B drugs: For example, amphetamines, Methylphenidate. Up to five years' imprisonment/fine for possession; up to fourteen years' imprisonment/fine for supplying.

Class C drugs: For example, anabolic steroids, tranquilizers. Up to two years' imprisonment/fine; up to fourteen years' imprisonment/fine for supplying.

Cannabis is usually smoked but can be used in food preparations. It makes the user relaxed and talkative. There is a whole debate surrounding the illegal status of cannabis. It has been classified as B then downgraded to C and is now class B again. Why all the fuss?

> Hang on! What about Cannabis?

> *I think cannabis should be legal. It is a natural plant and is less harmful than tobacco. It's no different to having a drink to unwind and relax. People have been smoking it for centuries, even religious people who claim that its effects help them achieve a higher spiritual awareness. It's daft making it illegal because it criminalises loads of people that use it and wastes police time. It's also known to have pain relieving effects. People should be able to make up their own minds.*

> *Cannabis should be class B. It is a dangerous drug. Long-term abuse can lead to mental health problems and increased risk of cancer, because it is mixed with tobacco. The use of cannabis also encourages people to try harder drugs for the rush, that's why it's called a gateway drug. Classifying cannabis warns people of the dangers.*

H – gear – skag – brown – smack – Mushies – microdots – dots – trips – tabs – Acid – Draw – weed – hash – puff – ganja – spliff – skunk – wacky backy – Trangs – moggies – maxxies – jellies – POPPERS – RAM – THRUST – ROCK – HARD – KIX – TNT – Speed – uppers – billy – phet – sulphate – sustanon 250 – Roids – anavar

40   Now you have begun to think about types of drugs

What do you think about this issue? Hold a class debate and take a vote?

The risks...why we stop, or don't start

Why we don't take drugs

> I sold the Christmas presents for my four-year-old, to buy drugs; my family kicked me out.

Ben, 22

> I got a criminal record for possession.

Sara, 19

> Sniffing drugs destroyed my nose. I had to have plastic surgery to hide it.

Jamie, 27

> Made me keep hallucinating. I still get panic attacks. Doctors say I've done permanent damage.

John, 34

> I weight train, and used steroids. Gave me road rage, no one could cope with me. I didn't like what I'd become.

Steve, 32

> My kid saw me shooting up.

Lynn, 24

> My mate fell into the canal. I was too gone to help. He drowned. I watched.

Lee, 15

> We had to sack her. She became too unreliable, even a risk.

Len, 48

> I've seen what it's done to my mates – it's not happening to me.

Gill, 27

> Just never been interested.

Dave, 26

> Seems a waste of money to me – gone in minutes with nothing good to show for it.

Sue, 18

Organisation Profile

Release was set up in 1967, and is the world's longest running drugs charity. It tries to provide a range of services dedicated to meeting the health, welfare and legal needs of drug users and those who live and work with them. They provide information and legal support. Check out their work at www.release.org.uk.

Release
Drugs, The Law & Human Rights

> There are lots of different types of risks to taking drugs – legal or illegal. Try to come up with a list of risks before you read those on this page.

Health risks – short- and long-term, disabling and fatal

If you desperately need a fix, you aren't going to check someone's HIV status before you share their needle, are you?

Financial problems – drugs cost money

If you are addicted, you need to take the drug, so the money has to be found. Hard drugs, such as heroin, lead people into hurting others to get the money they need. How do you cope when your mum steals your stuff to pay for her habit?

Uncertainty – you never know exactly what you are taking

Drugs are rarely pure. The side effects could include death. Did you really intend to pay for cement powder and cocaine?

Criminal risks

Getting a record can get you the sack, or restrict the jobs you can do. It can also be a block to travelling. How many parents would complain if they knew a teacher had a criminal record for drugs?

The Basics

1 Explain, using examples, how illegal drugs are classified.
2 Why do people take illegal drugs?
3 Explain, using examples, three ways that illegal drugs can harm a user.
4 In what ways do illegal drugs affect more than just the user?
5 **People should be free to use whatever drugs they choose.** Do you agree? Give reasons for your answer, showing that you have thought about more than one point of view.

The body and mind

In today's hectic world it is easy to forget how important it is to look after ourselves. Every year thousands of people have time off work or school because of illness, often when it could have been avoided if they had only listened to the warning signs their bodies were giving them. Lack of sleep, poor diet and misuse of drugs are just some of the ways people abuse their bodies.

All religious traditions teach that we are all special and unique in some way. This is summed up in the teaching of the *sanctity of life*. The physical body is seen as a shell that carries the real inner person. Within all religious traditions there are beliefs and practices that encourage believers to care not only for others, but for themselves. This means that where drugs are concerned, if they are for medical purposes most religious people would be happy to use them. However, for other drugs they would follow the specific teachings and guidance of their faith to decide if they are or are not acceptable.

> Make a list of ten things that many people do that are bad for their physical and/or mental well being.

Life is... A gift, Purposeful, Valuable, Precious, Holy/Sacred

 Buddhism

Health is the greatest of gifts (Dhammapada).

 Christianity

You should learn to control your body in a way that is holy and honourable (New Testament).

 Hinduism

Yoga destroys suffering for him who is moderate in eating, leisure activities, work, sleep and wakefulness (Bhagavad Gita).

 Islam

We give through this Qur'an all that gives health and is a grace to those who believe (Qur'an).

 Judaism

This [G-d's teaching] will bring health to your body and nourishment to your bones (Psalms).

 Sikhism

The pain of selfishness is gone. I have found peace, my body has become healthy (Guru Granth Sahib).

Research Task

Research some examples of religious beliefs and practices that help believers to keep a healthy mind and body. Use the headings in the Russian doll on the next page to help you.

Task

Now, write an information leaflet – Healthy Mind and Body: A (name of religion) Guide.

MORALITY – All religious traditions encourage people to live their lives honestly and with respect for others. This will help them to avoid conflict and achieve a sense of peace.

COMMUNITY – Being part of a faith community gives people a sense of belonging and **responsibility**. The community will also support people when they are having problems.

PRAYER – Regular prayers help believers to think about their values and what is important to them. They know there is always someone there for them when life gets hard.

MEDITATION – The practice of meditation helps to clear and focus the mind, helping a person to achieve a sense of peace and tranquillity.

CONFESSION – It can be very upsetting to do something wrong and have it weighing on your mind. Through confession, a believer can ease their **conscience** and demonstrate they are truly sorry. They may do this in personal meditation or seek the support of a religious leader.

DISCIPLINE – All religious traditions have rules and practices to encourage self-discipline. This may include not using drugs, performing daily rituals, going on pilgrimage and so on.

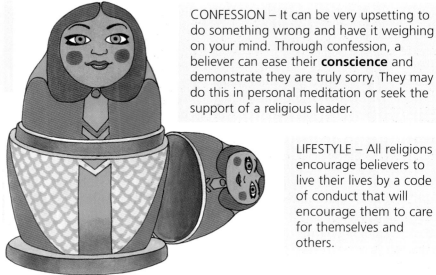

LIFESTYLE – All religions encourage believers to live their lives by a code of conduct that will encourage them to care for themselves and others.

How might religious belief and practice help someone have a healthy mind and body?

> *Find out about drug rehabilitation centres and their effectiveness.*

How can drug addicts be helped?

Lots of options are available, which include:

- Replacement drug therapies – addicts can be helped to get over withdrawal symptoms from addictive drugs, for example, by the use of nicotine patches, methadone and so on.
- Counselling – many addicts have underlying reasons why they use drugs. Support and guidance can help them resolve these issues.
- Voluntary self-help – groups like Alcoholics Anonymous are made up of people who have first-hand experience of addiction. Members support each other in their struggle to quit.
- **Rehabilitation** centres – specialist units run by health care professionals. These can be residential and use a range of treatments, therapies and counselling.
- Charitable organisations – many secular and religious organisations working with the poor and homeless also help addicts.

THE
PRIORY
The Priory Highbank Centre
Neuro Rehabilitation Services
Eating Disorder Service

✔ Now you have begun to think about health and well-being

Religious attitudes to drugs

Buddhism ☸

As a Buddhist, I am striving to reach enlightenment. This means that I should live my life according to the Middle Way that the Buddha taught. Anything that would cause me to stray from this path would not help me in my spiritual journey. The Buddha gave many guidelines on how to live life well and become enlightened. The Five Precepts advise me to not take drugs because they cloud the mind and would make it difficult to achieve enlightenment. They also remind me that I must not harm others and that under the influence of drugs many people do cause harm to others directly and indirectly. This is also why I do not smoke. Not only is it a health risk to me, but passive smoking harms others.

As a Buddhist I am free to choose my own path in life, but I prefer not to use any drugs including alcohol. The Pali Canon may be an ancient text, but we now know the dangers of alcohol that it refers to are very true. For example, loss of wealth, intelligence, health, morality and good reputation. Following the Eightfold Path I am reminded that the work I do must be positive and helpful, so I personally would not want to work in the tobacco or alcohol industry. The path also reminds me to have right awareness and meditation – using drugs would prevent me from doing this.

Christianity ✝

As a Christian, I follow the teachings of the Bible and the example of Jesus. There aren't any direct teachings saying drug use is wrong, so I rely on interpretations of the scriptures to guide me in the decisions I make. I would never want to use illegal drugs because they are harmful to myself and others, as well as being against the law, which the Bible says I should follow. Genesis tells me that God created me and that I am special and unique. St Paul says that my body is a temple of the Holy Spirit, so I should keep it sacred. Personally, I don't smoke because of the health risks, but I have Christian friends who do. I have also read that Rastafarians and people in the Ethiopian Coptic Church use marijuana as a means of heightening spiritual awareness, but this is an exception amongst Christians.

Alcohol is permitted in Christianity. St Paul advised his friend Timothy to drink some wine to aid his digestion and of course, wine is used during Holy Communion. In fact Jesus drank wine and in John's Gospel the first miracle Jesus performed was to turn water into the finest wine at a wedding in Cana. However, there are many teachings that warn against drunkenness and misusing alcohol. Proverbs says that getting drunk will just make you loud and foolish and Ephesians cautions that drunkenness will ruin you, so like many Christians I drink in moderation.

Task

All religious traditions accept drugs are necessary for medical use. They also teach that the law should be followed and so dealing in or using illegal drugs is wrong.

List some reasons why religious believers would:
1   Use prescribed or over-the-counter drugs (hint: benefits).
2   Not use illegal drugs (hint: consequences).

Hinduism 🕉

As a Hindu I live my life striving to achieve Moksha. This is release from Samsara, the circle of rebirth and suffering. To achieve this I must fulfil my Dharma, so I choose not to use drugs of any sort. My tradition does not say that I have to do this; there are no teachings against using drugs. Hinduism is a very personal spiritual journey; many Hindu holy men do use natural plant substances that have hallucinogenic effects to achieve a heightened spiritual awareness. This is only really practised amongst ascetics who have chosen to live a very different type of lifestyle, removed from the rest of society.

In modern Hinduism each person chooses for themselves if they wish to smoke or drink alcohol. The teachings do tell us, however, that anything which causes you to lose your mind is foolish and does not bring spiritual rewards. Meditation and worship cannot be performed correctly under the influence of drugs and taking them into a temple would be very disrespectful. If I am to succeed in life and follow a spiritual path I need to be healthy in mind and body.

Islam ☪

As a Muslim I do not use alcohol or illegal drugs as they are haram – forbidden. Prophet Muhammad (pbuh) called intoxicants the mother of all vices. The Qur'an says that my body is a gift from God and is on loan to me until Judgement Day. I have a responsibility to look after it and not abuse it with drugs. Drugs cloud the mind and are Khamr, which means to cover. The effects of illegal drugs would make it impossible for me to perform Salat (prayer) and meet my other responsibilities in life. Some of my Muslim friends do smoke tobacco, but are encouraged not to do this around others because of its harmful effects. Certainly, they must resist the temptation to smoke during Ramadan as it is forbidden to let anything pass through the mouth during daylight hours.

The Qur'an describes alcohol as the work of Sheitan. Prophet Muhammad (pbuh) once told a story of a man who drank and then proceeded to blaspheme, kill and commit adultery. The prophet said that whoever drinks, Allah will not accept their prayers for forty days. Many Muslims will not work where there is alcohol or enter a house where it is present. In Muslim countries there are very severe punishments for people who drink or are involved with any type of drug trafficking.

Task

1 What religious teachings would encourage believers to help drug addicts?
2 How might religious believers help drug addicts?
3 Research the work of a religious organisation that works with young people who are vulnerable to drug misuse and crime. For example, Centrepoint, Outreach for Youth, Street Pastors.

Judaism

Genesis tells me that I have been created by G-d and it would be wrong to do harm to His creation. My body is on loan and needs to be cared for until the Day of Resurrection. Illegal drugs would cause harm to my body and would also harm others. I have a responsibility to live correctly in society and contribute positively to my community. I could not do this if I were under the influence of drugs. I personally do not smoke, but I do have Jewish friends who do. However, it is harmful to yourself and others and many rabbis would encourage followers to avoid tobacco.

Alcohol is permitted in Judaism and wine forms an important part of many ceremonies. Every Sabbath the Kiddush cup, which contains wine, is blessed by the husband before being shared by the family. At Passover, four cups of wine are drunk. During Purim celebrations an ancient teaching that says get a little tipsy so you are unsure if you are blessing Mordechai or cursing Haman. However, our teachings also warn of the dangers of alcoholism and drunkenness. There are stories in the Tenakh which tell of how alcohol can make people fall into foolish and immoral behaviour. Wine is a gift from G-d, but it is to be enjoyed sensibly.

Sikhism

As a Khalsa Sikh I have made a commitment to avoid all tobacco, alcohol and anything that alters my body. The Kurahits prohibit any such things. When Guru Nanak was offered an opiate he replied that he was hooked on praising God. The Khalsa way of life requires discipline. Each individual must choose this path for themselves so the commitments made are an important part of achieving spiritual success. Using illegal drugs would damage the body and make the mind unfit for meditation on God's name. It would be wrong for any Sikh to use them.

The Reht Maryada tells a story about Guru Gobind Singh uprooting a wild tobacco plant.

When he was asked why he would do such a thing, he replied that if alcohol destroys a generation, tobacco destroys several. The dangers of tobacco are such that all Sikhs should avoid its use. As a Sikh my body is a temple for God and should be treated with respect. Alcohol can lead to sinful actions and it clouds the mind. A Sikh should be devoted to serving God and others and this requires a healthy mind and body.

Task

1 Explain, using beliefs and teachings, religious attitudes to:
   i. smoking ii. alcohol iii. illegal drugs.
2 **Religious people should not use recreational drugs.** What do you think? Explain your opinion.
3 **There is nothing wrong with people using drugs as long as they don't harm anyone else.** Do you agree? Give reasons for your answer, showing that you have thought about more than one point of view. Refer to religious arguments in your answer.

Now you have begun to think about religious attitudes to drugs

Exam practice

All questions in the exam are written to test your ability to respond to the assessment objectives (AO1 and AO2). The tips for answering AO2 questions are on pages 90–91. Let's take a look at AO1.

In AO1 questions you are being asked to show your knowledge and understanding of the topics covered. The questions will ask you to describe, explain and analyse the information you have learned.

The AO1 questions will add up to a total of nine marks. They can be broken up into a range of different mark allocations. There will be short answer questions of just one, two and three marks that can be answered in a single word, phrase or short paragraph. Some questions will be four, five or six marks and will need you to write longer answers, with more depth.

Sample <u>one-mark</u> questions – a simple word or phrase is usually enough.

1 Name an illegal drug?
2 Name a legal drug which is taxed?

<u>Two-mark</u> questions – these usually want a couple of different points, or the explanation of a single idea.

3 Give two reasons why some people use legal drugs?
4 What is meant by the term recreational drugs?

<u>Three-mark</u> questions – you will need to give a few different ideas, and a bit of explanation of at least one of them.

5 Explain why some drugs are legal?
6 Describe how illegal drugs are classified.

<u>Four marks</u> – these need three or more reasons, with at least two of those explained. If it asks for two reasons, you need to give a good explanation of each, not just a simple explanatory comment.

7 Explain two reasons why some religious believers would use caffeine.
8 Explain the possible consequences of using illegal drugs.

<u>Five marks</u> – again you need to give three or more reasons, and explain three or more of those reasons in some good depth. In depth means explaining an idea with two or three points.

9 Explain religious teachings about the use of alcohol and tobacco.
10 Explain the ways that religious believers might help drug users to kick the habit.

<u>Six marks</u> – at least three well-explained reasons are needed to get near to full marks. If the question is about religious attitudes, it is usually easier to write about two different religious traditions and get the full marks – because you have so much you can say, the same depth doesn't need to be there.

11 Explain why some religious believers approve of taxing legal drugs. Refer to beliefs and teachings in your answer.
12 Explain, using beliefs and teachings, religious attitudes to the mind and body.

Improving answers

You might think that when a test is over, that is it. Well, actually it can be a really good tool for improving your understanding and your exam technique. First of all, you could spot the things you missed, and make sure you learn them. Secondly, you could spot the bits of the test you were weakest on and go back to learning them once you have got a clear understanding. Thirdly, you can see where your technique let you down.

1 Name an illegal drug. (1 mark)

Caffeine – like in coffee

2 Explain two reasons why some people take drugs. (4 marks)

1 = To get well, because they are sick.

2 = Because it's their birthday and they are at a party.

3 Explain religious attitudes to alcohol. (4 marks)

Christians would say you shouldn't drink. It isn't the best for your health – mind or body. You might get carried away and do things that you wouldn't do normally. Then someone could get hurt or upset, like if you made a pass at your best friend's mate. You wouldn't normally do that, but the drink makes you. Christians do drink sometimes at Christmas and at Communion.

> This is part of Jimmy's test paper – it is only the AO1 questions. Check his answers. What mistakes has he made? How could he have improved his mark?

Exam technique – dos and don'ts

REMEMBER – there will also be AO2 questions on this topic. Here's a couple for you to have a go at. Look forward to pages 90–91 for some guidance.

4 **Drugs are a gift from God to be enjoyed.** What do you think? Explain your opinion. (3 marks)

5 **Alcohol and tobacco should be illegal.** How far do you agree? Give reasons for your answer. Refer to religious arguments in your answer. (6 marks)

DO

- Read questions carefully.
- Make your answer long enough to fit the marks on offer – a line and a half per mark in questions worth three or more is a good rule of thumb.
- Try to use a couple of quotes.
- Use good English.
- Check your answers.

DON'T

- Rush!
- Write the first thing in your head. Think.
- Move on to the next question after writing the first thing that came into your head – you might need more detail to get the marks.
- Assume the examiner understands anything you write – make it clear and spell it out.
- Worry if you can't remember the exact quote – write what you can remember.

Topic Four Religious attitudes to crime and punishment

This topic is about **law and order**. It is about what we mean by *crime*, why people commit crimes and the way society deals with offenders. It is also about why we punish offenders, and the debate about the death penalty. Key to the topic are religious teachings and beliefs about human nature, repentance and forgiveness. You will have to show your understanding of religious attitudes to crime and punishment.

ARSON ATTACK PUTS 500 PEOPLE OUT OF WORK

GRAFFITI ARTIST SENTENCED TO COMMUNITY SERVICE

POLICE ARREST DRUG TRAFFICKERS

GANGLAND SHOOTINGS SHOCK NEIGHBOURHOOD

VIOLENT CRIME ON THE INCREASE

DRINK DRIVER MAIMS SCHOOLGIRL AND GETS AWAY WITH A BAN

All societies have laws to guide people's behaviour. They should protect individuals, protect property and make society a safe place for everyone. When someone breaks the law they commit a crime. In the UK millions of crimes are committed each year. Many other crimes are not actually reported or followed up because they are considered trivial or the victim is too embarrassed or scared to say anything. Most crimes are committed by people under 25 years of age. Men are more likely to commit crimes than women. At some point in our lives most of us will experience the effects of crime.

There are two kinds of laws in the UK. *Bye-laws* are made by the elected councillors and apply to a local area. They cover things like parking restrictions, alcohol-free zones and environmental concerns such as litter and dog fouling. Breaking a bye-law can result in a fine, but you don't get a criminal record. There are also some strange bye-laws out there. For example, the law stating that it is forbidden to die in the Houses of Parliament was recently voted Britain's most absurd law.

Parliamentary laws are made by the government and apply to everyone in the country. These laws also put crimes into two categories. *Non-indictable offences* for example, minor crimes and driving offences. These are usually dealt with in a magistrates' court. *Indictable offences* are much more serious crimes. These are dealt with in criminal courts with a judge and jury.

Why do you think there are local laws and national laws – why not just one set of laws?

Most crimes fit into one of the following categories:

◆ *Crimes against the person* – offences causing direct harm to a person. For example, murder, rape, GBH.
◆ *Crimes against property* – offences that damage or deprive people of their property. For example, arson, burglary, trespassing.
◆ *Crimes against the state* – offences that potentially endanger everyone or affect the smooth running of society. For example, terrorism, drugs offences, perjury.
◆ *Crimes against religion* – not part of criminal law, but part of this course. These are rules set by religions, and only apply to that religion and its followers.

The Basics

1 Write a definition for all of the key words on this page (in italics).
2 Working with a partner, list as many crimes as you can think of. Now organise them into a table to show if they are a crime against a person, property or the state.

Causes of crime

Task

No one likes it when someone does something that hurts or upsets them, so why do people commit crimes? Make a list of reasons with a partner as to why you think people break the law.

What crimes are being committed here? Why might these people be breaking the law?

In your list you probably have lots of different ideas because there is no simple reason why crime occurs – if there was it would be easy to find a solution and put an end to crime and the misery it can cause. For some criminals, there is a trigger or immediate cause that leads them to break the law. For example, an argument in a pub might lead to a physical assault, or a group of bored youths may steal a car and go joyriding. However, there may be much deeper causes that lead, or even force, people into a life of crime. For example, a drug addict needs to pay for their habit. This might lead to theft, prostitution or drug dealing – all criminal offences.

It is important to know why someone commits a crime, because the punishment they receive needs to be effective. For example, a drug addict who steals is not going to just give up because they receive a fine or a short spell in prison. To prevent them reoffending they need help to overcome their addiction. If a murderer has deep psychological problems, there is no point locking them up in a regular prison where they will continue to be a danger to themselves and others.

Social reasons

Some people break the law because they may want to fit in with a 'gang' or are pressured by peers. They feel they need to 'show off' or prove themselves in some way.

Psychological reasons

Human nature may cause people to commit crime, for example, simply because they may be a greedy, aggressive or jealous person. Some people commit crimes because they have more deep-rooted problems such as sociopaths and kleptomaniacs.

Environmental reasons

Where people live and their home background can influence some people into crime. **Poverty** and deprivation have been linked with some criminal activities.

Drug addiction

Crime figures routinely show that drug addiction is the highest single cause of crime. Under the influence of alcohol or illegal drugs a person's judgement is impaired. Much 'gang' crime is drug related and individual addicts are often drawn into crime to fund their habit.

Now you have thought about why people commit crime

Crime and punishment exercise

Task

Look at the list of crimes below. Can you identify the name of the crime being committed in each case? Now look at the list of punishments available under the English law. What do you feel is the most suitable punishment in each case? For each one, say how you would punish the offender and why. What do you hope your punishment will achieve? Can you suggest any other punishments which you think would be more suitable?

Punishments

Life imprisonment

Fourteen years' imprisonment

Five years' imprisonment

Seven years' imprisonment

Two years' imprisonment

Six months' imprisonment

Suspended prison sentence (only enforced if they reoffend)

Community service

Curfew order

Anti-social behaviour order (ASBO)

Fine

Disqualification from driving

Attendance centre order

Electronic tagging

Probation order (required to meet probation officer weekly)

Restraining order

Exclusion order

Compensation order

Police caution

Crimes

1   A young woman who killed her husband after years of domestic abuse by him.

2   A man who raped two women.

3   A woman who assaulted a nurse who was treating her for a head injury she got while drunk.

4   A schoolgirl who stole items worth £65 from a department store.

5   Four football fans who kicked a rival fan to death during a street brawl after the match.

6   A schoolboy who covered a bridge near a railway station with graffiti.

7   A woman who defrauded £50,000 from her employers.

8   A person who sold drugs in a school playground.

9   A woman who drove her car for eight months without insurance or an MOT.

10 A student who did not purchase a TV licence.

11 A man who sexually abused a number of children.

12 Someone who set up a cafe for people to smoke cannabis on the premises.

13 A man who mugged at least seven people.

14 A gang of men who held up a train at gunpoint and stole millions in bank notes being taken for destruction.

15 A drunk driver who hit a pedestrian leaving them permanently confined to a wheelchair.

16 A man who killed at least nine people.

17 A young man who raped a woman he had been dancing with all night at a club and had walked home.

Task

Make a list of reasons why people who commit crimes are punished.

 Now you have begun to think about punishment

The aims of punishment

Society sets up rules, and we have to obey them or face the consequences. However, what one person thinks is very wrong, another person might consider less wrong. That is why we have a judicial system that sets tariffs for punishments to guide judges in the sentences they hand down.

A judge will also know other information before they give a sentence. For example, if the person has offended before, information from psychologists and perhaps about their home background. Would some of your decisions have been different if you knew more about the person?

> Did you think about the reasons why you were punishing someone in the exercise on the previous page? How might this have influenced the decisions you made? There are six main aims of punishment and you probably came up with all of them in the punishment exercise.

Vindication

People who break the law must be punished; otherwise there is no point in having the laws in the first place. If there were no penalties for breaking the law there would be little motivation to keep it. For example, someone who parks in a car park and does not display a valid parking ticket may get a fine, because the rule says you must have one. It doesn't matter that the car park is nearly empty, you are only going to be ten minutes and you don't have change – rules are rules and we can't choose which ones we are prepared to follow.

Deterrence

A punishment is meant to be unpleasant so that the offender is put off committing crimes in the future. A burglar who gets sent to prison for five years will hopefully not want to experience that again. Also, if we know what the punishment is going to be, many would be put off committing the crime in the first place. For example, the penalty for drink driving in the UK is a minimum

twelve month driving ban, a hefty fine and potentially a prison sentence, so most people don't do it.

Protection

Some criminals pose a danger to people and society in general. The laws exist to protect people and their property. One way this is done is by locking up criminals who commit serious offences such as murder, child abuse and arson. In some cases criminals are housed in special prisons for those with serious psychological problems that mean they are unlikely to ever be able to conform to the laws of society.

Retribution

This is taking revenge on the offender; simply put, it means 'getting your own back'. When people break the law, someone somewhere is almost always hurt, even if they are just upset or angry. Most people follow the law so it isn't fair that a few criminals want to just ignore the rules and do as they please. Society uses punishment to make the offender pay for what they have done. In some cases **retribution** can be very severe. In the UK criminals can receive lengthy prison sentences; in other countries they use capital or corporal punishment.

BRING BACK HANGING FOR MURDERERS

Reformation

Obviously society cannot simply lock up everyone who breaks the law and throw away the key. Many punishments are given to try to change the nature of the person who has offended (**reform** them). This is because most people who break the law are going to still be part of society. It is important to try to make these people realise the effects their action had on others and then hopefully they will not do it again. For example, someone convicted of joyriding might have to do **community service** in a physiotherapy unit dealing with victims of road traffic accidents. In prisons there are usually education and work programmes to support offenders in their rehabilitation. This helps to prepare them to rejoin

society as a constructive member. Religious groups especially feel this is an important aim of punishment.

Reparation

Reparation means to make up for what you have done. Someone who breaks the law must be made to make amends and compensate their victim or society for their wrongdoing. For example, if an offender damages property they may be made to pay for the damage they have done to make up for the hurt and inconvenience their actions have caused. In the UK, as well as the criminal courts there are also civil courts. These often deal with cases where one person or group will 'sue' another for the damage or injury they may have incurred because of the other's negligent, selfish or criminal activity. For example, a person who injures themselves at work may sue their employer.

COMPANY ORDERED TO PAY RECORD DAMAGES TO INJURED WORKER

The Basics

1 Explain each of the six aims of punishment.
2 **Protecting people from criminals is the most important aim of punishment.** What do you think? Explain your answer.

 Now you have thought about the aims of punishment

Punishment

Look at pages 52–53 on the aims of punishments. What aims are met by each of these punishments?

Punishments in the UK	
Custodial sentences	**Locking the offender up**
Prisons (adult)	There are different categories of prison in the UK. High security prisons are category A and B and house the most dangerous offenders; category C prisons are used for those serving shorter sentences; and category D are open prisons for first time offenders and those due to be released.
Institutes for the criminally insane	Used to house offenders with serious psychological disorders who are a threat to the safety of others and themselves, such as psychopaths and sociopaths.
Young Offenders Institutions	Used to house offenders classed as children (under 18 years of age). Routines specifically targeted at children's needs.
Non-custodial sentences	**Alternatives to prison**
ASBO	Anti-social behaviour order sets restrictions that the offender must stick to e.g. curfew, not go to certain places.
Community service	Must do unpaid work in the community, for up to 240 hours. They do not have a choice although their offence and experiences may influence magistrates.
Curfew	Must return home by a set hour, often used with tagging.
Electronic tagging	An electronic device attached to their leg that means their movements can be monitored.
Fines	A set amount of money must be paid for the offence.
Probation	Offenders must meet regularly with a probation officer who monitors their behaviour.
Restorative justice	Young offenders must attend sessions where they look at their crime, why it was wrong and its effect on the victim.

FACT! Prisons spend on average just £1.85 on each inmate's daily food

FACT! 80% of inmates cannot complete a basic job application form

FACT! 2 suicides each week in UK prisons

I work for the Prison Reform Trust and have direct experience of how damaging locking people up can be. It's easy to say that prison life is easy when you have never been inside one. The reality is very different. Conditions in some prisons are very poor; inmates can be locked in their cells for 23 hours a day. Problems such as over-crowding, lack of exercise, poor diet, boredom, violence and drug abuse are a daily experience. I think it is really important that prisoners have the opportunity to reform and the hope of reward for good behaviour.

FACT! 71% of all prisoners suffer 2 or more mental disorders

Parole means that a person can be released early, having served some of their sentence. When on parole they must live within the law and are supported by a parole officer, who will help them to reintegrate into society. The parole order may require them to have treatment, for example, for drug abuse. The aim is to help them avoid reoffending and become active and purposeful members of society.

I'm in this young offender's institute coz they want to change me, reform they call it. I have to go to sessions and talk about the stuff I've done and how it affects others. I've done loads of stuff. I've had warnings, three ASBOs, paid fines and done community service a couple of times too. I didn't do the last one though coz it was boring. I'd have gone if it was working on cars or something like that. Me and the gang like TWOKing and hanging out in the street. I'm only in here coz a copper saw me flashing me blade. I miss home and me mates and I'm well fed up with all the rules.

CT! It costs £41,000 keep a person in prison for 1 year

The Basics

1 Describe the long- and short-term effects of prison sentences on the offender.
2 Make a list of the advantages and disadvantages of non-custodial sentences.
3 Explain three reasons why young offenders are dealt with differently to adults.
4 **A life sentence should mean life in prison.** Do you agree? Give reasons for your answer, showing you have thought about more than one point of view.

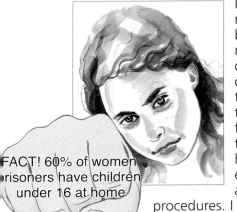

I'm doing two months in prison because I allowed my teenage daughter to stay off school. I didn't think it would come to this. I was so frightened when they brought me here and embarrassed by the admittance procedures. I cried constantly for the first three days. It is hard to adjust to having your life run by someone else. I can't stop worrying about the kids. My mom isn't well so they have had to go into foster care. I know I'm going to lose my job too, because they don't know I'm in here, unless they have read the local papers. Going home will be really bad, everyone will know and they probably think I'm an awful mother.

FACT! 150,000 children have a parent in prison

FACT! 60% of women prisoners have children under 16 at home

FACT! March 2007 saw 2500 under 18's being held in prisons

I was imprisoned twenty years ago for armed robbery. It wasn't my first offence, I had done time before. I thought it was important to be hard and to stand up for myself. I got into a disagreement with a prison warden and ended up with another sentence for GBH. I should have been paroled by now, if it wasn't for that. Somehow it just doesn't seem important anymore. My wife divorced me by mail a few years back. Joey and Tina were just toddlers when I was sent down. I didn't see them grow up. I sometimes wonder what they are like now. Simple things like having a beer in the pub, driving a car, cuddling on the sofa are just distant memories. I'm used to life in prison, the routines, not having to make decisions and I've learned to just do as I'm told!

Organisation Profile

The **Prison Reform** Trust was founded in 1981. It works to create a more humane and effective penal system. It provides advice, information, educational work, research and campaigning. Its work has been very effective in achieving change in prisons, as well as in the policies and practices of the penal system. Find out about this charity through its website at www.prisonreformtrust.org.uk.

 Now you have begun to think about the effects of punishments

Capital punishment

Capital punishment is the death penalty. In most countries this is reserved for the most extreme offences, usually murder. Worldwide, other crimes such as blasphemy, adultery, drug offences, corruption, fraud, smuggling, treason, hijacking and war crimes are capital offences.

> *Are any crimes so bad they merit the death penalty? What do you think?*

Why use such an extreme punishment?

The crimes are seen as so bad that no other punishment would be suitable. Society must take revenge on the individuals who commit such heinous acts and deter others from committing such offences. It is the principle of 'an eye for an eye' and is seen as the *law of equality of retribution* in Islam. A murderer shows no respect for human life, so the state has none for theirs. Many holy books name certain offences as being punishable by death.

USA Executions (1997 to 2008)	
Lethal injections	930
Electrocution	153
Lethal gas	11
Hanging	3
Firing squad	2

In 1977 the USA allowed individual states to choose if they wished to use capital punishment. Presently 34 states have readopted the death penalty – Texas is responsible for over one-third of all executions that take place. To date there have been over 1127 executions in the USA. Right now there are over 3300 people awaiting execution in America's death row cells. Amnesty International has said that the USA is savage, barbaric, cruel, prejudiced and uncivilised. This is because the USA has executed: people who offended as a child; people who have mental illnesses; blacks sentenced by all white juries where the prosecution has removed potential black jurors from trials; where reasonable doubt has been shown to exist; where defence had been inept; and foreign nationals who have been denied the help and counsel of their own governments.

Check out more about the death penalty in the USA at www.amnestyusa.org.

Facts and figures

- 110 countries have abolished the death penalty in law or practice.
- 85 countries retain and use the death penalty.
- This century 88 per cent of all known executions have taken place in China, Iran, Saudi Arabia and the USA.
- Between 1990 and 2003 the USA executed 15 children (under the age of 18 at the time the crime was committed) – more than half of those executed worldwide.
- In March 2005 the USA abolished child executions, affecting over 70 juvenile offenders on death row in 12 states.
- In the USA, since 1973, over 99 prisoners on death row have been released after their convictions were overturned.
- Methods of execution worldwide include: firing squad, hanging, lethal injection, stoning, beheading, gas chamber, electric chair, crucifixion (Sudan).
- This century over 17,000 people worldwide have been recorded as executed by their governments.

> *Discuss the information above. What issues does it raise about the death penalty?*

Did you know? Over 900 people have been killed by lethal injection in the USA, some of them dying in excruciating pain. Victims have been seen gasping for air, convulsing, grimacing in agony and have received chemical burns a foot long. Some executions have lasted as long as an hour.

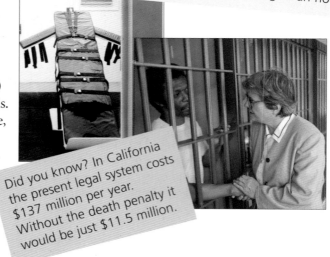

Did you know? In California the present legal system costs $137 million per year. Without the death penalty it would be just $11.5 million.

Find out more about the work of Sister Helen Prejean and the move to abolish capital punishment in the USA. Watch the film *Dead Man Walking*.

The arguments for capital punishment

◆ An 'eye for an eye, life for a life' means that murderers should pay with their life.
◆ Deterrence – to put people off committing horrendous crimes.
◆ **Justice** for the victims and their families.
◆ Life sentences do not mean life; murderers walk free after a few years.
◆ Terrorists murder indiscriminately and they cannot be reformed.
◆ It's a waste of resources housing criminals for their entire life.
◆ It's natural law; the death penalty has been used for centuries around the world.
◆ It demonstrates that society will not tolerate some crimes.
◆ This is the only way to totally protect society from the worst murderer who cannot be reformed.

The arguments against capital punishment

◆ Retribution is uncivilised; two wrongs don't make a right.
◆ Most murders are done on the spur of the moment, so capital punishment would not deter.
◆ Victims' families still grieve; killing the murderer doesn't end the pain of loss.
◆ It is a contradiction to condemn murder and then execute (kill) a murderer.
◆ Executing terrorists would make them martyrs.
◆ Legal systems can fail and innocent people can be executed.
◆ All life is sacred and murderers should be given the chance to reform.
◆ It is inhumane and degrading to put anyone through the mental torture of death row.
◆ Legal systems are full of inequalities and prejudices.

Should the UK reintroduce hanging?

Organisation Profile

Amnesty International

Amnesty International was founded in 1961 by Peter Benenson, a British lawyer. Today it is the world's biggest human rights organisation, informing the world about human rights abuses and campaigning for individuals and political change. Amnesty disagrees completely with execution, seeing it as cruel, inhumane and degrading. In its reports about the death penalty in the USA, it has highlighted the degrading nature of the system, giving examples of prisoners being taken from intensive care to be executed, wiring up prisoners who were still awaiting last minute appeals, executing people who were clearly mentally ill, and a paraplegic being dragged to the electric chair. Campaigning against and monitoring the use of the death penalty worldwide is just one part of Amnesty's work. The organisation campaigns to end all human rights abuses and recognises the inherent value of all human life. Find out more about Amnesty International by checking out their website at www.amnesty.org.uk.

The Basics

1 What is capital punishment?
2 Explain three reasons why some countries use the death penalty.
3 Use the information from pages 59–61 to explain religious attitudes to the death penalty.
4 **It is never right to execute a murderer.** Do you agree? Give reasons for your answer, showing that you have thought about more than one point of view. Refer to religious arguments in your answer.

Human nature

To understand religious attitudes to crime and punishment, it is helpful to first consider what they teach about human nature. Laws exist to control behaviour and make society work. But do they assume anything about what people in general are like? Which of the following do you most agree with?

a. People naturally try to be good and act in a way that will make others happy.
b. People are naturally selfish and will act in a way that will make them happy.
c. People are neither good nor bad, their actions are shaped by their experiences.

All religions have rules and laws that believers must follow. This shows us that they believe people need some sort of framework and guidance to help them live their lives correctly to achieve their spiritual aims. For example, the Ten Commandments apply to Jews and Christians, and Sikhs follow a code of conduct called the Reht Maryada. When a believer does something that breaks one of their religious laws they commit a *religious offence*, this is sometimes called a *sin*. Just like in society when someone breaks a law they are punished, there is also the belief in religious traditions that believers who sin will be punished in some way. Ultimately their afterlife could be affected – going to hell or being reborn in a lower life form.

Deciding what is right and wrong can be a tricky business. Religious people have several sources of authority to guide them. They should, however, always be guided by their *conscience*. This is sometimes described as the voice of God inside your head telling you what is right or wrong. Have you ever felt guilty, ashamed or disgusted with yourself because of a wrong action? Conscience is what causes these feelings.

Religious traditions accept that everyone makes mistakes, but they also teach the ideas of *repentance* and *forgiveness*. To repent is to recognise that we

Codes of Conduct Holy Books
Conscience
Councils
Tradition Upbringing
Spiritual Leaders

have done something wrong and to be truly sorry. It involves learning from the mistake and doing our best not to repeat it. Forgiveness is accepting that a person is sorry for what they have done wrong and allowing them a second chance.

Religious people are also guided by *duty* (things that must be done) and *responsibility* (understanding we are in control of our own actions). They have duties and responsibilities to themselves, others and (except for Buddhists) God. Correct living means self-discipline and putting others first. Human nature then, can be developed and guided for good in the world. Fulfilling your duties and responsibilities leads to spiritual rewards in the afterlife.

Task

Find out about the main law codes of the religions you are studying.

The Basics

1 What is meant by the terms: right and wrong; human nature; religious offence; sin; conscience; repentance; forgiveness; duty; responsibility?
2 How is the behaviour of religious people guided by their faith?
3 **Religious people should always forgive wrongdoers.** What do you think? Explain your opinion.

Religious attitudes to crime and punishment

Buddhism ☸

Buddhism teaches that people should follow the laws of the country in which they live. The Noble Eightfold Path relates to living life correctly. Each of the steps in the path starts with the word 'right' and they emphasise the importance of correct action. A life of crime would not be right livelihood and criminal activity would be against the First Precept because it causes harm to other people. Furthermore, the motivation behind crime is often linked to selfish human traits and desires. Breaking the law would lead to bad karma and this would affect future rebirths, preventing a person from achieving enlightenment.

Buddhist teachings:

- Suffering is caused by attachment to the material world.
- The three poisons (greed, hatred, ignorance) are the cause of evil actions.
- The law of karma – the sum total of good and bad actions.
- Buddhists should practice Metta (loving kindness) and Karuna (compassion).
- The story of Milarepa illustrates that all people are capable of change.

Buddhists teach that all people can change and bad actions will have karmic consequences. Buddhists would agree that the public needs to be protected from dangerous criminals. However, imprisonment should provide opportunities for the offender to reform and be helped not to create further bad karma. The principles of non-harming and compassion mean Buddhists would not agree with punishments that were unduly severe or would cause direct harm to the offender. The Angulimala society provides support for prisoners.

Christianity ✝

Christianity teaches that the laws of a country should be followed unless they are unjust. The Ten Commandments are reflected in the laws of the UK. St Paul taught that the state should be obeyed because God has given permission for it to exist. For Christians, law breaking means they are committing sins as well as crimes. This could affect them in the afterlife because they believe they will be judged by God. In Roman Catholic Christianity there is also the belief in purgatory. This is a place of suffering and torture where souls must be cleansed before they can enter heaven.

Christian teachings:

- 'Love your neighbour' (Jesus) – Christian love (agape) should be shown to all people.
- Pray for those who persecute you (Jesus).
- The Ten Commandments – A law code that guides behaviour.
- Forgive your brother 70 x 7 times (Jesus) – meaning that a Christian should always be prepared to forgive those who wrong them.
- The Lord's Prayer – recognises that everyone sins and needs forgiveness.

Christians accept that offenders must be punished. Punishments should be fair and just and offenders should be treated humanely. The Quaker Elizabeth Fry devoted her life to prison reform. Amnesty International, which was founded on Christian principles, works worldwide to campaign for the protection of prisoners' human rights. The story of Adam and Eve (The Fall) shows that everyone sins. Christians believe that people should have the opportunity to repent for their wrongdoing and make amends. It is important to follow the example of Jesus and be prepared to forgive others. Most Christians do not agree with the death penalty. Some, however, follow the Old Testament teaching of an eye for an eye.

Task

1 Look up the stories of Angulimala and Geshe Ben. What do they teach about Buddhist attitudes to crime and punishment? www.angulimala.org.uk

Task

2 Look up the Parable of the Lost Son and the story of the woman caught in adultery. What do they teach Christians about repentance and forgiveness?

Hinduism ॐ

Hindus believe that all people should follow the law and that rulers have a responsibility to ensure justice is carried out and people are protected from offenders. In the Hindu scriptures dharma (duty), caste and the belief in karma are important influences on attitudes to crime and punishment. Every Hindu is born into a caste and has a duty to fulfil. Criminal activities bring bad karma and would cause a person to be reborn into a lesser life form. The principle of ahimsa (non-violence) would also be broken, since crime causes harm to others physically and/or emotionally.

Hindu teachings:

- Karma – all evil actions result in bad karma that influences rebirth.
- Reincarnation and moksha – the cycle of rebirth (samsara) depends on karma. Moksha can only be achieved through good actions.
- 'An eye for an eye makes the whole world blind' (Gandhi).
- 'When a person claims to be non-violent...he will put up with all the injury given to him by a wrongdoer' (Gandhi).
- Murdering a Brahmin is the most serious of crimes (Laws of Manu).

Hindu teachings make clear that just punishments should appropriately provide retribution, deterrence and reformation. In the past the severity of punishment was greater the lower the caste of the offender. In modern times many Hindus follow the example of Gandhi and would expect offenders to be treated humanely and that punishment should make provision for the offender to learn from their mistake and reform. The Laws of Manu make clear that the death penalty is acceptable for crimes such as murder, theft and adultery, but in India today only murder and treason are capital offences.

Islam ☾

Muslim law (Shari'ah) is both secular and religious. It is based on the Qur'an, Hadith and Sunnah of the prophet. An offender therefore breaks God's laws as well as man's law. To outsiders Islamic law can appear to be extreme. However, Islam is a complete way of life and all Muslims have a responsibility to each other and the community. For example, there is no reason to steal because Zakat is provided for the poor. Criminal activity is an offence to God and will be punished on earth and in the afterlife.

Muslim teachings:

- A thief, whether man or woman, shall have their hand cut off as penalty (Qur'an).
- The woman and man guilty of adultery or fornication, flog each one of them (Qur'an).
- We ordained for them; life for life (Qur'an).
- Day of Judgement – Allah will decide who goes to paradise or hell.
- If a man is killed unjustly, his family will be entitled to satisfaction.

Crime in Islam can be divided into four groups. *Hadud* – the worst crimes: murder, blasphemy, theft, adultery, false accusation, treason, highway robbery and drinking alcohol. There are capital and corporal punishments for these offences. *Jinayat* – involve killing or wounding and the victims have the right to claim compensation. Offenders can pay Diya (blood money) as part reparation for their crime. *Ta'azir* – are lesser crimes and punishments are decided by a judge who will consider social pressures and change. *Mukhalafat* – covers laws related to the smooth running of the state such as driving offences and a judge decides the punishments. Punishments should ensure that justice is served. Islam accepts there may be mitigating circumstances to be considered and allows for the forgiveness of offenders.

Task

1 Find out how Gandhi led a campaign of peaceful civil disobedience against British rule in India. Write a report on your findings.

Task

2 Find out more about the use of capital and corporal punishment in Islamic countries. Write a report on your findings.

Judaism ✡

The Torah is the Jewish law book and includes 613 *mitzvoth* (rules). These outline the conduct expected of all citizens. They include secular and religious guidance. All Jews are expected to follow the law and keep their religious duties and responsibilities. There is also guidance on repentance for wrongdoing. Jews believe that G-d will forgive and be merciful if a wrongdoer makes *atonement* – repents their sins and makes amends. They can do this through prayer, fasting and charitable giving. The *Bet Din* – Jewish court makes decisions about religious matters.

Jewish teachings:

- The Ten Commandments.
- G-d created the world with justice and mercy so that it would last (Midrash).
- The Lord does not enjoy seeing sinners die, He would rather they stop sinning and live (Neviim).
- If anyone takes the life of a human being they must be put to death (Torah).
- Yom Kippur – the Day of Atonement when Jews make confession and atonement for sins.

Judaism teaches that society should be protected and that people should be deterred from committing crimes. Punishment should be just and rehabilitate the offender. The Torah does allow execution for some crimes and emphasises the need for corroborative evidence from two independent witnesses. The teaching of an 'eye for an eye' is about making amends. The death penalty exists as a deterrent and it is rarely used, Judaism considers it important for offenders to have the opportunity to atone for their crimes.

Task

3   Look up the Ten Commandments. Explain how they guide religious and secular behaviour.

Basics

Use pages 59–61 to explain the attitude of the religions you are studying to:
1   the law
2   punishment of offenders
3   capital punishment.

Sikhism ☬

Sikhs regard the law as important for ensuring justice and the protection of weaker members of society. All people need God's guidance to avoid the evils of anger, greed, lust, pride and attachment to worldly possessions. Human nature means that sometimes people fall into sin, but they should have the opportunity to repent and make up for their mistakes. Khalsa Sikhs follow a strict code of discipline (reht maryada) when they commit to the community. If a Sikh were to break this code they would have to make reparation before the rest of the community. In society, Sikhism teaches its followers to be law abiding, but to be prepared to fight against injustice and oppression.

Sikh teachings:

- Law of karma – evil actions result in bad karma and lower rebirth.
- Kurahits – religious vows guiding personal conduct.
- Kirpan – a symbol of the fight for justice and truth.
- 'If someone hits you, do not hit him back, go home after kissing his feet' (Guru Granth Sahib).
- 'He who associates with evildoers is destroyed' (Guru Granth Sahib).

Sikhs believe in *nirvair* – trying to be without hatred. They accept that it is important to punish criminals in order to protect society and reform the offender. They do not accept physical or mental torture, as they respect the dignity of all human life and the essence of God within all. Many Sikhs support human rights organisations like Amnesty International and would offer support and counselling to convicts. Sikhs are told to follow their conscience and many would not support the death penalty because of the belief in the sanctity of life. However, some may regard it as a useful deterrent and just punishment for some crimes.

Task

4   Look up the Sikh kurahits. Write a report on how they would influence a Sikh's life.

Exam practice
Time test

As you get near to the exam it is important to practise writing timed answers to the exam question. You need to allow time in the exam to settle down, read the paper and have time to check through your answers at the end of the exam. This means you have about twenty minutes to complete a question. Remember to look at the marks available for each part of the question. They will help you to judge how much you need to write and therefore how long to spend on a question. If the question is worth one mark, you don't need to write a five minute essay!

It is important not to rush through your answers; you do have time to complete them well. It is worth spending a few moments thinking about your answer to a question before actually rushing to write it down. Some questions are only short answer responses and will not take very long. Questions asking you to describe, explain or give opinions and reasons will take more time. These questions will need you to think through your answer first; it might be worth making a few pencil notes planning your response if it's a question you're finding difficult.

Exam Tip

Stimulus material is provided to help you orientate your responses so it is worth spending a few moments studying the material provided. In the question below, the picture provides a direct link to a couple of the questions. Can you see which ones? How can the stimulus help you to write a good response?

TAKE THE TIME TEST – *complete the exam question below in twenty minutes.*

Religious attitudes to crime and punishment

a. Give **two** examples of a crime against property. (2 marks)

b. Explain why some people commit crimes. (3 marks)

c. 'Religious people should never break the law.' Do you agree? Give reasons for your opinion. (3 marks)

d. Explain religious attitudes to the death penalty. (4 marks)

e. 'The most important aim of punishment is to protect people.' Do you agree? Give reasons for your answer, showing that you have thought about more than one point of view. Refer to religious arguments in your answer. (6 marks)

Sometimes it's easy to write loads more than you need, and to get the question wrong, or to write too little. So here is some guidance to help you with the time test from the previous page.

Question guidance

a. (**2 marks**) Questions require only a couple of words, phrases or sentences in response.

There are lots of possible ideas here, notice the question asks for **two** crimes so naming each will be enough. Make sure that the **two** you give are against property not just any crimes.

b. (**3 marks**) The question asks for explanation so it is important to make sure that you develop each of the ideas you use. Just listing the reasons is not explaining them and so will not achieve full marks. It is a good idea to write a reason and then say why it causes someone to commit a crime. Not only does this make your answer clear for the examiner, but it also helps you to make sure you have done what the question asks. Again there are lots of possible ideas here but, make sure your answer is based on reasons rather than opinions.

c. (**3 marks**) Here the question is asking for your opinion on an attitude expressed in the statement. You may agree with, disagree with, be undecided or even have no strong opinions at all. Whatever your response, it is important to remember that your opinion must be supported by reasons. A reason is different to an opinion because a reason can be supported with evidence. There is a difference between emotional opinions and informed opinions. In the exam you need to write an informed opinion using two or three reasons to be assured of full marks.

d. (**4 marks**) Here the question is going to need you to spend a few moments structuring your answer. It is worth jotting down any quotes you are going to use in your answer. You need to write a clear and cohesive account to achieve full marks. Rambling answers can be overlong and cost you time in the exam, they are also not necessarily going to achieve full marks.

In this question you need to write about religious attitudes to the death penalty. There are several ways to approach this. One possible way is to think of the response as two paragraphs. In the first paragraph you say why the death penalty would not be agreed with by the religion you are studying. In the second paragraph, you say why they would, in some cases, support the use of the death penalty. This will depend on the religion you have studied. Make sure you make direct reference to at least two religious teachings or beliefs. You can use quotes or paraphrases and you do not have to say exactly where they come from.

Don't worry if you can't remember everything – you can still achieve full marks for an answer if it is clearly and coherently written, including some of the main points.

e. (**6 marks**) The full evaluation part always comes last in the question. It is worth spending a few moments planning a structure for your answer and even briefly jotting down a couple of reasons for and against. You will also need to include reference to at least one religious viewpoint, so it can be worth jotting down any ideas you have for that too. Remember you are evaluating the attitude expressed in the statement NOT the topic in general.

In this question you are being asked to weigh up the different aims of punishment. You need to present reasons that both agree and disagree with the idea that protection is the most important aim of punishment. It's a good idea to also include examples to support your reasons. Think about the victims of crime and the dangerous nature of some criminal actions to find reasons to support this statement. To disagree, think about the other aims of punishment, and religious attitudes to repentance and forgiveness. It's always a good idea to make sure you break your answer up into at least three clear paragraphs. You should finish by stating what your opinion of the statement is, with a reason or two.

Topic Five Religious attitudes to rich and poor in British society

When we think about rich and poor, we don't necessarily think of people in Britain. We assume most people are fairly wealthy and if not there is plenty of help available both from the government and other organisations. However, although there are less extreme problems than in less developed parts of the world, problems do exist.

In this topic we will look at the issue of the causes of wealth and poverty in Britain, how people gain wealth and indeed lose it. Secondly, we will focus on attitudes to money from the point of view of the six world religions. Thirdly, the course will have a look at responses to this issue and who is responsible for helping such people in Britain.

So let's get started... Let's look at some possible causes of poverty in Britain.

Homelessness

On the streets of our cities a growing number of people sleep rough. According to the charity *Crisis*, there are some 380,000 **homeless** and it is heading for one million by 2020. This includes 'The Hidden Homeless' – people who sleep rough, squatters, people who sleep on other people's floor, people in hostels and so on. So why is the problem increasing? The cost of housing in Britain has risen dramatically over the last twenty years and social housing (council houses) have been sold off.

In London 500 hostel beds are used every night by the young homeless, many of whom left home because of difficult family situations, abuse or they simply did not feel wanted. They get involved in crime to survive, often drug/alcohol abuse and leave education. 60 per cent are black or from other ethnic groups. Many have mental health and behavioural problems. They cannot get a job because you need a fixed address and to get a fixed address you need a job! Many homeless people are ex-armed forces. When they leave they find they cannot cope with an ordinary job or home life and end up on the streets. It is estimated that the homeless problem costs £1.4 billion a year, in lost taxes and schemes to help.

Task

Research homelessness in Britain. Search Google or use these websites to start you off: www.shelter.org, www.news.bbc.co.uk, www.aquilaway.org, www.wsws.org/articles.

Produce a leaflet, PowerPoint® or organise a class debate on the issue. You could think about the following statement: 'In Britain, the world's fourth richest country, nobody should be homeless'.

Gambling

As people have become more affluent in Britain more people have become involved in **gambling**. Some are serious gamblers and others might just have a 'flutter' on the odd occasion. However, at the other end of the scale, there are many people who are poor and use gambling as a way of winning money. The problem is that for every occasion they win, there are many times when they don't. Also when someone does win there is the buzz to carry on. In the long run this gets them into a far worse financial situation, but the chance of winning big money keeps them gambling.

> So why do people gamble?
> What kind of things do people gamble on?

It is probably true to say that it is possible to gamble on anything. Traditionally, sport was the focus.

All major events now have 'odds' on them happening or their outcome – you can bet on anything that does not have a guaranteed outcome. Remember that there are casino complexes now, poker on the TV, bingo halls and online betting.

Venue for next Olympics · Snow at Christmas · Next Premier League manager to lose his job · Next number one hit · Winner of Premiership · Winner of music award · **Gambling** · Grand Prix winner · Name of next royal baby · Next Prime Minister · Who is marrying/divorcing who · Next celeb to have a baby · Next US President · Winner of X Factor · Christmas No. 1 is...

The Basics

1. Explain what is meant by gambling.
2. Explain why people gamble, using examples.
3. Describe three ways people can gamble
4. **Gambling is always wrong.** What do you think? Explain your opinion.
5. **Gambling is an addiction for all who do it.** What do you think? Explain your opinion.

Religious attitudes to gambling

Task

Using the teachings below explain what you think the religious attitude/s would be to the following gamblers:

1 A person who once a year puts a £10 bet on the Grand National Horse Race.
2 A person who is addicted to gambling and gambles everyday, whether they have the money or not.
3 A person who needs the money from gambling to pay off debts.
4 A person who puts £10 on the lottery twice a week every week.

Buddhism

- Craving (tanha) associated with gambling and wealth will not bring true happiness.
- Wealth should he earned honestly (right livelihood).
- We need wealth to meet our needs but no more in case we become attached to it.

Islam

- O you who believe, wine and gambling...are filthy tricks of Satan; avoid them so you may pray.
- The profit from gambling is less than the sin gained. It is haram.

Christianity

- Gambling denies the biblical work ethic that associates honest labour with deserved reward.
- A greedy person is an idolater who cannot obtain salvation. (Gambling implies greed).
- The love of money is the root of all evil (New Testament).
- Some accept fundraising by raffles and some agree the lottery is fine in moderation.

Judaism

- Money should be earned from working – doing G-d's work on earth.
- The motive of gambling is greed. It is not forbidden but the spiritual consequences are a worry.
- Gambling does take place as part of festivals (Purim).
- Playing the lottery is fine in moderation.

Hinduism

- Uncontrolled pursuit of wealth will result in unhappiness.
- One should only accept those things that are set aside as his or her quota.
- Some do see the lottery/gambling in moderation as acceptable.

Sikhism

- Kirat-Karni – means earning ones money by honest means including labour. The Guru Granth Sahib says money should not be spent on gambling and drinking.
- Two of the five major vices – Lobh (greed) and Moh (worldly attachment), lead to gambling or are fed by gambling.

Now you have to learn to apply teachings directly in answering a question.

 Now you can give a top answer to a question on gambling!

Other causes of poverty

It is true to say that many of the problems that leave people in poverty are linked – many people are affected by more than one factor that leaves them in poverty.

Task

1 Read the following descriptions from people's lives and decide what the cause of poverty in each situation is, the effects of this and who the blame lies with. You might find that although there is one main cause in each statement there are secondary causes and effects too.

My name is David. I've been on the streets for 'bout two years. I've no money – left home with nowt – mum don't care! It's cold. Need to get warm. I do drugs to take away my thoughts – it feels good, blocks out the world. Nothing to look forward to – I'm on my own, it's up to me.

My name is Joe and I'm 44... Had a heart attack last year and now can't work much. I don't get a lot in benefits because they say I am not that bad – but they don't really know how I feel. I am frightened that it could happen again if I do too much. I am too young to die. I can't afford much (no luxuries) so I really struggle.

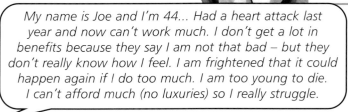

I'm called Becky – I am 14. I live at home with my dad and his girlfriend. I have a brother and two half-sisters. Dad got made redundant and now only works part-time so we haven't got much. Perhaps if he didn't smoke and drink so much I might have been able to go on the school trip! He does try I guess but I never have trendy clothes and feel ashamed when I'm with mates. I try at school coz I want a better life than this. I want stuff for my children.

I'm Jason. School was a waste of time – couldn't be bothered with all that stuff. Teachers just shout and you can't do what you want. Didn't go to many lessons – skived off with mates. Didn't do homework – stupid after being at school all day! Most days didn't get up till 11 – liked lying in bed better. Now I'm unemployed – claim job seekers allowance but it ain't much. Can't buy stuff I want but don't want a job either.

My name is Claire. I had to help mum when I was young so I missed a lot of school – she sent me out shopping 'coz she couldn't be bothered. Now I can't get a decent job with money, can't read much and don't have any confidence to do stuff.

Task

2 As a class, discuss the issues you raised when looking at the five statements. For example, what about this issue of blame? Does this make a difference to whom and how we are prepared to help?

Poverty is a complex issue, one with many causes, but the effects of those suffering from it are difficult to solve. In Britain when poverty happens there is alongside it the issue of blame. Whereas poverty in, say, developing countries is usually not a matter of blame – natural disasters and weather, for example, cannot have real blame attached – some people think that poverty in Britain is usually caused by a person's actions or inactions. They might say 'Well if they hadn't done...' or 'It's their own fault because...' or 'It's their choice to be...' and so on. Despite this blame issue we still have a responsibility as individuals and as religious people to help people in such situations.

So now you know all about some causes of poverty

Where do people get their wealth?

Business and enterprise

Many people earn their wealth from the businesses they run. A good education has set them up well to start their own business. They have worked hard at a trade and been successful. Some people might be entrepreneurs – designed something new and made a fortune from it. Hard work has paid off and money has been made.

Gifts and inheritance

Others might be wealthy by virtue of the family they were born into or have received money through **inheritance** (money left them in a will on the death of someone).

They have wealth through no efforts of their own. However, the person who gave the money may have earned it through hard work.

Earnings and savings

A person may have a good job and have been paid well. They have earned their money. Perhaps they have been careful and invested money or saved it. The question is, of course, the job that earns them that money. Does a premiership footballer *do enough to earn* their living? Could it be argued that a nurse, for example, works much harder but earns much less and deserves more? On the surface it appears fine to *earn* money but with the above example, does it matter *how* it is earned?

Dishonest means

These *are* other ways that people become wealthy. However, none of these are ways that people *should* be making themselves wealthy. Wealth is gained at the expense of the suffering of another.

Exam Tip

Let's do some evaluation questions on this topic.

a. **It does not matter where a person's wealth comes from.**

b. **It is better to earn money than to inherit it.**

c. **If you give to charity it does not matter how you earned your money.**

d. **Jobs in the caring profession should earn the most money.**

Think about how to agree and disagree with the above statements. They are all asking whether it matters where money comes from or whether if you use wealth in the right way this makes up for where it comes from. The same ideas could be used for them all. You just need to be able to adapt them. Discuss the questions in pairs – jot down some ideas in bullet points. Keep it simple and remember it for the exam.

So now you know the causes of wealth

Religious attitudes to the poor and to the use of money

For the exam you need to know what the religious views are on money and giving to the poor. The issue of money is about how people earn their money or where their wealth comes from. It also focuses on how people view and use money in their lives. Is it more important than anything else? Does the quest for money rule peoples' lives? Is it about greed and selfishness?

With regard to the poor in Britain, the exam will focus on religious attitudes to the different groups of people who are poor for the various reasons we looked at earlier. The general response is that, from a religious perspective, we should help anyone in need, regardless of whether it is their fault that they are in such a position. We are not here to judge. Judgement will come later, either from God or in the process of rebirth. All you have to do is to learn some teachings to support this view. It is as simple as that!

Buddhist attitudes

Buddhism believes that there is essentially nothing wrong with wealth but the issue is about how it is used.

- Riches ruin the foolish...through craving for riches, the foolish one ruins himself (Dharmapada).
- Acquiring wealth is acceptable if, at the same time, it promotes the well-being of the community or society (Phra Rajavaramuni).
- Unskilful thoughts founded in greed are what keep us circling in samsara, in an endless round of repetitive, habitual attachment (Kulandanda – a leading member of the Western Buddhist Order).

Buddhism encourages right action, right thought, right intention and right livelihood. Therefore, to see poverty and ignore it would be wrong. Buddhists have a duty to help the poor.

- Dana (charity or generosity) is part of the basis of merit making that the Buddha taught.
- Karuna (compassion) is wishing others to be free from suffering.
- 'In our world today everyone is looking for personal happiness. So, I always say, if you wish to be happy and aim for self-interest, then care for others. This brings lasting happiness. This is real self-interest, enlightened self-interest' (Dalai Lama).

Christian attitudes

Christians believe that there is nothing wrong with wealth in itself; it is how we use that wealth which is important. We can use it for good and bad. If we have wealth, it is seen as a gift from God. Our money should come from lawful means. In the Bible there is the warning that the wrong attitude to money could lead people away from God.

- People who want to get rich fall into temptation and into foolish and harmful desires that plunge men into ruin and destruction. The love of money is the root of all evil (New Testament).
- No one can serve two masters...You cannot serve both God and money (Bible).
- Be on your guard against all kinds of greed: a man's life does not consist in the abundance of his possessions (New Testament).

Christian believe that whatever the reason for a person being poor, we have a duty to use our wealth to help them. It is not our right to judge but to help.

- Go sell everything you have and give it to the poor and you will have treasure in Heaven (New Testament).
- If anyone has material possessions and sees his brother in need how can he love God? (New Testament).
- What good is it if a man claims to have faith but has no deeds... If a brother has no clothes or food what good is it to wish him well without caring for his physical needs? (New Testament).

Hindu attitudes ॐ

Rich devotees are not to hoard wealth, but to operate as a steward and distribute that wealth. It is important to create wealth (artha) to provide for family and maintenance of society. A requirement for religious living is to share wealth. There is a danger of excess wealth as it leads to overindulgence and a materialistic rather than a spiritual life.

- Money causes pain when earned, it causes pain to keep and it causes pain to lose as well as to spend (Pancatantra).
- Happiness arises from contentment, uncontrolled pursuit of wealth will result in unhappiness (Manu 4).
- 'Act in the world as a servant, look after everyone and act as if everything belongs to you, but know in your heart that nothing is yours – you are the guardian, the servant of God' (Shri Ramakrishna).

Hindus believe that life is all about good deeds here and now. This not only helps the individual but it helps their own rebirth.

- Some believe that by helping those in poverty (even if it is their own fault), they can improve their own karma and rebirth.
- Hindus have the principles of Daya (compassion) and Dana (giving to charity).
- It is taught that 'it is the same God shining out through so many different eyes. So helping others is no different than helping ourselves'.

Islamic attitudes

In Islam to be wealthy is to be given a gift from Allah. We, as humans, are caretakers of Allah's wealth. We will be judged by the use of it.

- Riches are sweet, a source of blessing to those who acquire them by the way – but those who seek it out of greed are like people who eat but are never full (Hadith).
- To try to earn a lawful livelihood is an obligation like all other obligations in Islam – no one has eaten better food than what he can earn by the work of his own hands (Hadith).
- It is not poverty which I fear for you, but that you might begin to desire the world as others before you desired it, and it might destroy you as it destroyed them (Hadith).

Islam teaches that wealth comes from Allah for us to use it to benefit humanity. If we have wealth it is a test for us to see what we do with it. The Pillar of Zakah commands us to help the poor.

- He who eats and drinks whilst his brother goes hungry is not one of us (Hadith).
- If the debtor is in difficulty give him time to pay – but if you let it go out of charity this is the best thing to do (Qur'an).
- Zakah (the Third Pillar) gives an annual payment to be used for worthy causes as well as a special Zakah on Eid ul Fitr. Sadaqah is giving voluntarily to charity.

Exam Tip

Think about the following questions:

1 Using beliefs and teachings, explain why religious people help the poor in Britain.

It could be that this type of question is focused on one type of poor in particular, as in question 2.

2 Using beliefs and teachings, explain why religious people should help the homeless.

It might have asked about drug addicts or those who are lazy or people who have gambled money.

3 Using beliefs and teachings, explain attitudes to the use of personal wealth.

Make sure you actually apply the teachings to the topic. Students often just include teachings in their answers without showing any understanding of them.

Judaism attitudes

Judaism believes that wealth is a gift from G-d and can be used for the self and others. The Tenakh clearly states that money can only be earned in the correct way. Materialism can lead to people sinning – if your heart is filled with the desire for money then there is no room for G-d. The Talmud does, however, see that a decent standard of living is needed for the well-being of the individual.

- Do not weary yourself trying to become rich (Proverbs).
- He who loves silver cannot be satisfied with silver (Ecclesiastes).
- He who has a hundred, craves for two hundred (Midrash).

Money is not desired but it is necessary. A Jew is expected to look after their home and give to the poor. Even the poorest of people can give something. The giving of Tzedakah (correctness) is not seen as charity because it is not a matter of doing someone a favour: it is giving the poor what is rightfully theirs.

- 'You shall not burden your heart or shut your hand against your poor brother' (Torah).
- It is forbidden in the Torah to charge a fellow Jew interest on money.
- The Talmud suggests that anyone who can afford it should give to the poor cheerfully, compassionately and comfortingly.

Sikhism attitudes

Sikhs also believe that a person who possess riches is blessed by God by virtue that they are able to help the poor. Livelihoods should be made by honest means. Anything that is earned dishonestly is seen as the 'blood of the poor'.

- One who lives by earning through hard work, then gives some of it away to charity, knows the way to God (Guru Granth Sahib).
- Be grateful to God for whose bounties you enjoy (Guru Nanak).
- Those who have money have the anxiety of greed (Adi Granth).

Sewa (service to others) is a distinctive aspect of Sikhism. Guru Nanak thought Sewa was a way of teaching man humility and a sense of responsibility to all those in need. It is also an act of worshipping God. It is obligatory for all Khalsa Sikhs as a duty. At the langar, a community meal is served for any who want it – Sikh or not. In Indian gurdwara, tens of thousands of meals a day are given free.

- The sign of a good person is that they always seek the welfare of others (Bhai Gurdas).
- A sign of divine worship is the service of one's fellows (Bhai Gurdas).
- A place in God's court can only be attained if we do service to others in the world (Adi Granth).

Exam Tip

There are a whole range of teachings in this topic but for revision purposes you don't need to know that many. Make sure you know the general teachings from the front of the book and learn either two of the above if you are studying one religion or one from each if you are studying two religions.

Try writing on a piece of paper two teachings on each subject for the four courses you are studying. Put it up somewhere so you can take a look every so often. You will be surprised how quickly you know them off by heart.

 So now you know the religious teachings on attitudes to money and helping the poor

So what do we do to help in Britain?

If we accept that poverty exists in Britain then, as a developed, democratic country, we should have things in place to help. In fact help comes from many areas – charities and religious organisations, the state government, and direct help.

Many charities in Britain work for the people of Britain. They find it hard to raise money, probably because they don't have major disasters to publicise with heart-rending pictures of suffering. At the same time there are many people who believe that if you are in Britain and poor then you only have yourself to blame and do not deserve any help.

Shelter was founded back in 1966, but the need for housing advice and assistance has never been more vital than today in Britain. Shelter is the largest of the UK housing charities. The charity was formed in the slums of London where founder Bruce Kenrick realised that while the rich were getting richer, the number of poor families in the UK was spiralling. Shelter has often suffered from a lack of mainstream exposure as people can't believe that so many people are struggling today. The sad truth is that more and more families are falling into the poverty trap.

Shelter

www.shelter.org.uk

Shelter has many fundraising initiatives. One well-known activity was 'Strip for Shelter' in 2003 where students, office workers, etc., paid £1 to wear a football shirt for the day.

The Salvation Army? Yes it's those people who we see at Christmas in shopping centres playing music and with collecting tins! They actually work all year round:

- Rebuilding lives – offering a hand-up to homeless people, a family tracing service, drug and alcohol rehab, anti-human trafficking services.
- Comfort and support – food parcels, lunch clubs for older people, supporting the emergency services during major fires and incidents, visiting prisoners.
- Belonging – kids and youth clubs, music groups are some examples.

As a Christian Church and registered charity, The Salvation Army also runs a Christmas Present Appeal each year for children, the homeless and older people who would have little or nothing at Christmastime. It runs homeless resettlement centres, care homes for older people, employment services for the long-term unemployed, support services to the armed forces, and home visiting services in local communities. All this is done by volunteers and ministers who believe in putting their Christian beliefs into action – to follow Jesus' example to help (not judge) anyone who is in need.

Gamblers Anonymous is a fellowship of men and women who share their experience, strength and hope so that they may help themselves and others to recover from a gambling problem. The only requirement for membership is a desire to stop gambling. It is estimated that more than 250,000 people have a serious gambling habit in Britain today.

So now you know about the charities who work in Britain

Government help

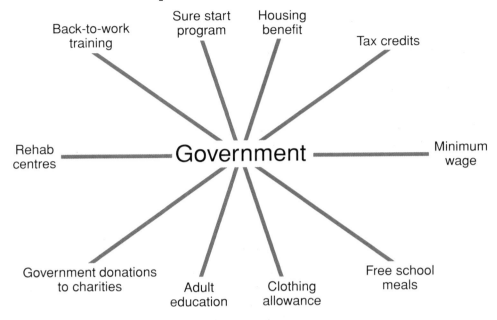

Back-to-work training · Sure start program · Housing benefit · Tax credits · Rehab centres · **Government** · Minimum wage · Government donations to charities · Adult education · Clothing allowance · Free school meals

COUNSELLING · WORK TRAINING · DRUG REHAB CENTRE · ALCOHOLICS ANONYMOUS · GAMBLERS ANONYMOUS · ADULT LITERACY & NUMERACY PROGRAMME · PERSONAL FINANCIAL MANAGEMENT PROGRAMMES · CITIZENS ADVICE BUREAUX · JOB RETRAINING · SMALL BUSINESS SUPPORT · CONNECTIONS FOR CAREERS ADVICE · APPRENTICESHIPS · ¿¿¿¿¿

The spider diagram is looking at what governments can do for the poor, whereas the picture is looking at what decisions can be taken by those in poverty to help them improve the situation that they are in.

Task

Thinking about the options available, answer the following questions:

1 Explain where people in poverty can get help from.
2 Is it better to accept the help available or initiate recovery from poverty yourself?
3 Why might some people not claim the government help available?

Key terms you need to know...

There are two key terms that might be specifically referred to in your exam: **minimum wage** and **excessive salaries**.

The minimum wage is the least amount of money an employer can legally pay a worker per hour. It is set by the government. Currently it is £5.73 for people aged over 22; £4.77 for 18–21; and £3.58 for under 18s. (Figures as of 1 October 2008).

So why is this a good idea? Why would religious people support this?

Well, firstly it protects workers at the lowest end of the pay structure from employers trying to exploit them as 'slave labour', as it is commonly known. Secondly, it protects British workers from foreign workers who are willing to work for much less. Thirdly, it protects the employers from workers challenging their pay. Religious people believe in fairness and the idea of a fair day's work for a fair day's pay. The only real downsides are that, for example, when a young worker reaches 18 they might find an employer trying to get rid of them in order to bring in another under eighteen so they are able to pay less. In Britain a person is an adult at the age of eighteen and could therefore have the same rights and responsibilities as a 22-year-old (family, for example) so why should age make a difference to how much they are paid? From a business point of view a company might not be able to employ as many people because of financial constraints.

At the other end of the pay spectrum is the issue of excessive salaries. These are salaries that are very high in relation to the job that is being done. Is a footballer worth £100–150,000 per week plus bonuses for winning and sponsorship deals? In the city, top workers earn millions and company bosses often have exorbitant salaries and get paid bonuses whether the company is doing well or not. At the same time, workers are often given a pay rise that is below the level of inflation. This raises the problem of value for money for the work done. Also there are other people doing very valuable jobs who are paid much less, such as nurses. However, others would argue that they are at the top of their respective professions, they have worked hard to get there or they have a special talent. If the country wasn't willing to pay such salaries these people would disappear to countries that are willing to pay them.

Who should care about the poor?

An MP   Charities   Families   Religious communities   Poor people   Tax payers   Businesses

Task

Explain why the people in the pictures above have a responsibility to care for the poor.

Do you think some have more responsibility than others?

How much responsibility lies with the poor person themselves?

You've just won £6.4 million...

Now that's serious money! This is what a lottery win could do for you – make you very, very rich! That is why people play it – a win would make a very real difference to their lives. There are lots of arguments regarding the issue of gambling on the lottery. The fact that it is just about luck and involves no skill or hard work is a problem for some people. To others it isn't really gambling; they see it as a game, a bit of fun.

> Think about the statements below.
> What issues do they raise about the lottery? In pairs write down your ideas.

> The lottery makes people millionaires. I think the prizes should be less so that the money is spread out amongst more people.

> The issue is not about gambling; it is about what you do with the money. If you help family, friends and give to charity then this justifies the gambling.

> It is too much money to win – it gets spent on wasteful things.

> It would change my life – how can you carry on as normal with so much money – new friends, begging letters, everyone wants something off you... I just want a normal life.

> I would buy a big house, flashy car, have a luxury holiday, oh and go shopping to fill my wardrobe.

> Winning the lottery will answer all my problems.

> Winning big would make anyone happy – you can do whatever you want now.

> The chances of winning are slim...people spend more than they can afford and this gets them into further debt.

> Having discussed the issues would you want to win the lottery? Why?

> How would a lottery win help these people? How would they spend it, do you think?
> Do you think they deserve it? If only one could win who would you think deserved it the most?

For religious people there are still issues with the lottery – greed, selfishness, wasting money, materialism versus spiritualism, people winning at others' expense, tickets you cannot afford, misuse of money.... But the lottery does have a positive side – giving money for good causes, helping families, giving people opportunities, giving money to places of worship, having the ability to make a real difference.

This is an interesting topic with plenty of scope for questions to be asked about it. You need to be able to think and discuss both sides of the argument – and you just did! So you are prepared for the exam now if you learn the issues!

Now you know about the lottery

Exam practice – what the grades look like

1 'Religious people shouldn't gamble'. Do you agree?
  Give reasons for your answer, showing you have
  thought about more than one point of view.   (6 marks)

Now to get all six marks, you'd have to answer from two points of view. You'd have to give two or three reasons for each side, which you had explained. You'd also have to include at least one religious argument.

Candidates for each grade write in a certain way – on reading a script, experienced examiners can often make a good guess at what the grade could be because of the style used by the candidate. That is to say, there are characteristics that can be recognised in each grade. Here we use that evaluative question to showcase the characteristics of grades A, C and F.

	Candidate answer	Comment from Examiner
F	I agree because you should earn your money by hard work. I disagree because it is up to you what you do with the money you have earned – it's your money!	This is a simple response, with no development. It does make a point for each side of the argument, but only very simply. The next step this candidate could make to improve their grade would be to increase the number of reasons they give.
C	I agree because by gambling you are wasting money because you very rarely win anyway. It just gets you more into debt and you could spend the money on more sensible things. Religion tells us to earn money honestly. I disagree though because with the lottery if you don't win some money goes to charity anyway.	C-grade answers generally give a spread of ideas. They are often light on good development, or are one-sided. They lack depth or breadth to their answer. They give some religion, but again it lacks development and depth. If quotations are used, they aren't used to their full potential. Reading it, you get the impression that they have a clue, but could have said so much more. The next step this candidate could make to improve their grade would be to increase the number of reasons they give.

	Candidate answer	Comment from Examiner
A	On the one hand, some people might agree with this statement because essentially gambling is against religious beliefs. Religion tells us to earn our money honestly and when money becomes more important than anything else then there is a serious problem. Christianity teaches us that the love of money is the root of all evil. It can lead to many social problems like further debt because you lose more than you win. It can lead to family break-ups because of serious addiction and families losing everything they have. On the other hand, gambling may not always be wrong for religious people. It can be a bit of fun, for example a £2 bet on the Grand National. If it is in moderation then it does no harm. The Bible does not condemn it outright. Also, with the lottery, religious people may see this as acceptable because money from it goes to many charities so even if the person does not win, good comes of the money.	A-grade candidates provide both sides of an argument, and they include religion. They explain the points they make, often applying the points they make to the statement. There is breadth and depth to their answers – on both sides. Their answers flow, and are easy to read as well – often the examiner can see it is worth five or six marks before they even reach the end of it! Of course, they'll read it all, but the structure stands out, and helps the examiner with their marking.

Have a look at some of your answers to evaluative questions. What sort of answers do you give? What does the next level do that you don't?

Here are some questions for you to try:

2 **Religious people should help the poor**.
Give reasons for your answer, showing you have thought about more than one point of view. (6 marks)

3 **Getting huge wages encourages greed**.
Give reasons for your answer, showing you have thought about more than one point of view. Refer to religious arguments in your answer (6 marks)

4 **Homeless people have chosen that life, so religious people should not help them**.
Give reasons for your answer, showing you have thought about more than one point of view. (6 marks)

Exam Tips

Learn the DREARER formula for good evaluative responses:

Disagree with the statement

Reasons why you disagree

Explanations of some of those reasons

Agree with the statement

Reasons why you agree

Explanations of some of those reasons

Religious argument must be in there

Don't get fazed – it isn't that hard to get four or more marks for these – just follow the formula.

Topic Six Religious attitudes to world poverty

Having looked at the issue of rich and poor in Britain in the last section, we now move on to the topic of world poverty. Although at first glance this can be seen as being a very similar subject area, the reasons why it is happening and what it involves are totally different. So, what do we mean by poverty in the world context?

When most people talk about poverty they think about money or indeed the lack of it! However, when we are looking at *world* poverty it is a far more complex issue. The pictures above might give you some clues as to what is involved. The focus for this course is on the areas of the world commonly known as less economically developed countries (**LEDCs**). Many of these countries are south of the equator, have high populations which are growing, have an issue with their climate, are prone to natural disasters, have been (or still are) ravaged by civil wars, have massive national debt and are exploited by richer nations. In such countries the issue is about survival and what people need simply to stay alive.

What do you need to know?

You will need to understand the key issues that cause poverty in LEDCs, religious attitudes to poverty and how the religions and religious believers try to help, the work of charities with long- and short-term aid, **world trade** and **global interdependence**. These are interrelated problems all contributing to world poverty.

Task

Find out which countries are categorised as LEDCs. This will be useful as you start to understand the causes of poverty.

Key Concepts

In relation to world poverty and how religion responds to it there are three concepts to know:

- Justice – the idea that people have a right to be treated fairly, in this case by the sharing of wealth.
- Stewardship – the responsibility to look after the world and everything in it, particularly those who are poorer than us.
- Compassion – the ability that humans have to be affected by the suffering of others and want to care for and help them.

The basic needs of life

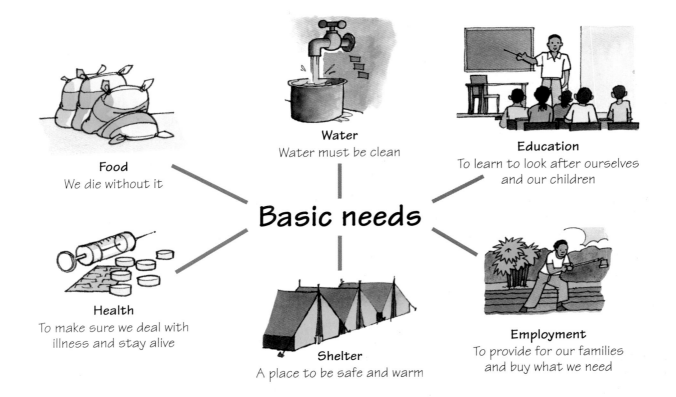

Food
We die without it

Water
Water must be clean

Education
To learn to look after ourselves
and our children

Basic needs

Health
To make sure we deal with
illness and stay alive

Shelter
A place to be safe and warm

Employment
To provide for our families
and buy what we need

Fact File

- 1 in 8 people in the world do not have enough to eat – many survive on one simple meal a day.
- Too many people do not have access to clean water – millions die every year from drinking dirty water.
- Only 1 child in 4 has access to secondary education in developing countries – many girls remain illiterate.
- Three-quarters of the people in developing countries have only limited access to doctors and medicine.
- Many homes have no running water or electricity and many people are homeless.
- Real jobs are sparse; many live off what they grow.

The Basics

The following tasks can be done in groups. Each group is given one of the six basic needs of life. Put the word in the middle of a large sheet of paper.

1. Write down three different reasons why people need it/need access to it.
2. Write down three ways help could be given to solve the problems caused by the lack of it.
3. In terms of the six basic needs and how important they are to our survival, from 1–6, what position would you put the topic your group are dealing with? Explain why.
4. If your group had unlimited money, which of the six needs would you focus on? Why and what would you do?
5. Each group could report back as to the decisions they have made.

For a homework task you could research your topic for some actual statistics from developing countries to learn the key issues.

 Now you know about poverty and what makes someone poor

So what causes all this poverty across the world?

Climate

Many countries suffering poverty are situated near the equator – Africa, Central and South America, India, the Middle East and South and East Asia. The climate of such areas has a massive effect on peoples' lives. Many places are very hot and rainfall is minimal – many months seeing no rain at all and yet when it does rain, it is so hard that the land floods. Land is dusty, little grows and people go hungry because the crops fail. The lack of water at all, and clean water in particular, means that disease spreads.

Added to this are environmental problems – global warming and climate change. Recently in Britain and Europe we have experienced climate problems such as droughts (leading to bans on using hosepipes or washing cars) and severe floods (leaving people homeless and businesses ruined). The difference is that we have the means to cope. Imagine having no food for your family because nothing grows, nothing to sell at market, no clean water to drink because the rivers and lakes have all dried up, diseases and hunger spread, animals cannot feed, dry land all around, and no government help for these difficulties. In the rainy season too much water arrives too quickly – the land floods, homes are destroyed and people killed. This is a year on year problem.

Natural disasters

The poorest countries in the world are at risk of the worst natural disasters. These are caused by a natural occurrence which we cannot control. Environmental experts say that through global warming and pollution, man is having an impact on nature itself. Recent examples include droughts in Ethiopia, floods in Bangladesh, a hurricane leading to flooding in Burma, an earthquake in Pakistan and the Tsunami in the Indian Ocean. Floods in particular are a real problem; the countries are too poor to prepare for them or deal with them alone when they happen. Usually they result in thousands of deaths. The countries rely heavily (not through choice) on aid from rich nations.

Exam Tips

To get a good grade you must be able to *apply* these teachings. It does not matter what area of poverty is stated in the question, the passages you can use (probably three) will be the same.

Buddhism

- Karma – the belief that our actions will affect our rebirth.
- Ahimsa – the idea that nothing should suffer.
- Dana – charity or generosity. Part of the basis of merit making that the Buddha taught.
- Karuna – compassion. This means wishing others to be free from suffering.
- 'I always say, if you wish to be happy and aim for self-interest, then care for others. This brings lasting happiness. This is real self-interest, enlightened self-interest' (Dalai Lama).

Christianity

- Jesus told us to 'love thy neighbour'.
- 'Treat others as you wish to be treated'.
- Jesus said to a rich man 'go sell all you have and give to the poor then you will have treasures in heaven'.
- If a rich person sees his brother needs help, he should help him. If he does not then he cannot claim to love God.
- The Parable of the Sheep and Goats – it is those who have helped others that are rewarded in heaven.

War

War is a major contributory factor to poverty. In many LEDCs, even if we just focus on the last 30–40 years, there have been unstable governments, infighting causing internal civil wars and wars between poor countries. War causes poverty in two main ways. Firstly, the money spent on weapons costs millions of dollars – money that should be spent on improving the lives of the countries' people. Whilst many people suffer extreme poverty the governments of some of these countries are actually very rich. They just don't spend money in the right areas. Secondly, war destroys crops, homes, schools, hospitals and families. People flee their own country and become refugees, which also puts pressure on other poor countries.

Corruption

In many LEDCs one of the key issues is corruption. This is firstly at government level. Usually the government has not been democratically elected by the people of the country. It has come to power by force or civil war and it is kept in power by the support of the army. Many of these governments are brutal regimes. They take the wealth of the country and spend it on weapons, keep themselves in power through bribery and fear, and spend huge amounts on luxuries for themselves. People who oppose the governments usually disappear without trace. Examples of such corruption would be President Amin in Uganda and, more recently, Robert Mugabe in Zimbabwe. On a local level, council officials are equally as corrupt. All this means that the people of the country are left very poor and with no means to change the system that keeps them poor.

The Basics

1 Give three causes of poverty.
2 Explain the attitude of one religion to someone who lives in poverty.
3 **Natural disasters are the main cause of poverty.** What do you think? Give reasons for your answer.

Hinduism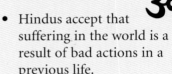

- Hindus accept that suffering in the world is a result of bad actions in a previous life.
- By helping those in poverty, people can improve their own Karma and rebirth.
- Daya (compassion) and Dana (giving to charity).
- 'It is the same God shining out through so many different eyes. So helping others is no different than helping ourselves'.
- 'Act in the world as a servant, look after everyone; you are only the guardian, the servant of God' (Shri Ramakrishna).

Islam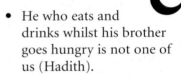

- He who eats and drinks whilst his brother goes hungry is not one of us (Hadith).
- Allah rewards us in heaven for our good deeds.
- If the debtor is in difficulty give him time – but if you let it go out of charity this is the best thing (Qur'an).
- Zakah (the Third Pillar) gives an annual payment to be used for worthy causes. Sadaqah is giving voluntarily to charity.
- Muhammad (pbuh) set the example in the early Muslim community to share with each other.

Debt

Many LEDCs have to borrow money from banks or the World Bank. This money allows them to start to develop. However, the interest that has to be paid is very high and quite often the interest payments are higher than the foreign currency they earn from the exports they make. Hence their national debt is always increasing. In July 2005 at the meeting of the G8 (the world's richest countries) in Edinburgh, decisions were made to try to help this situation. It was stated that reductions in debt payments would be made to countries that allowed democratic elections to take place. This was the proviso because over the last twenty years massive amounts of money have been poured into Africa in particular, and yet much has gone into the pockets of their corrupt military leaders rather than helping the people it was aimed at.

Fair Trade and exploitation

Small-scale farmers in developing countries grow vegetables and fruit for their own consumption and keep animals for meat, milk and eggs. Many also grow export crops such as tea, coffee, rice, fruit and cotton as their major source of cash income. It is difficult for most of these small farmers to trade their goods on the global market, because international trade rules are weighted in favour of rich countries. This keeps small farmers in poverty. Products carrying the **FAIRTRADE** mark are guaranteed to have met international standards ensuring those in developing countries who produced them received a better deal, including a fair price for their work and an additional sum to invest in community projects.

The other issue here is **exploitation** of workers. Often multinational companies have their products made in LEDC's. The point of this is that workers in these countries are prepared to work for sub-standard wages because it is better than nothing. Women, and indeed children, work in sweatshops and factories many hours a day, in very hot conditions, where they have no workers rights and are paid less than 30 pence a day! Much of what we wear and what we eat are produced in these conditions. What do you think religion would say about this?

Are we prepared to pay more so that people can earn a respectable wage or do we just buy these products without giving a thought to their origins?

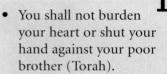

Judaism

- You shall not burden your heart or shut your hand against your poor brother (Torah).
- It is forbidden in the Torah to charge a fellow Jew interest on money.
- Amos suggests that if you skimp on a measure, boost the price, cheat the scales and so on, G-d will not forget.
- The Talmud suggests that anyone who can afford it should give to the poor cheerfully, compassionately and comfortingly.
- He who pursues righteousness and kindness will find life and honour (Proverbs).

Sikhism

- Dhan (part of Sewa) means service to humanity by giving to charity and giving time to help people in need.
- There can be no worship without performing good deeds (Guru Granth Sahib).
- Heaven is not attained without good deeds (Guru Granth Sahib).
- After you shall depart this life, God shall demand a reckoning of your deeds that in his ledger are recorded (Guru Granth Sahib).
- Vand Chhakna – encourages Sikhs to live generously, and Daswandh – giving a tenth of surplus wealth to serve people, for example, for famine or other disaster relief.

So now you know all the religious attitudes to helping the poor

So where are the LEDCs?

These countries are mainly situated south of the equator in Africa, Asia and South America. However, over the last 30 years these areas of the world have seen different rates of development. There are 49 countries that are classed as less economically developed. Within this number some are the *'least developed'* where there is extreme poverty, civil war, political corruption, Aids epidemics, low incomes and human resource weaknesses; these are economically very vulnerable places such as Ethiopia, Rwanda, Tanzania and Uganda. There are also some countries with *'emerging markets'* such as Brazil, China, South Korea, Egypt.

Task

Tough decisions

Imagine that you run an aid agency. This year you have collected just over £2 million. How would you respond to the following requests? The country where it takes place is important. Is it a least developed or an emerging economy? Does it make any difference to your decision? Think about how much money you have to spend and what that money could be spent on. Be realistic and prioritise!

Our village is a shanty town just outside the centre of Sao Paulo in Brazil. We have no running water, and many of our young people have died due to dirty water. Our houses (made out of what we can find) are cramped and we have no electricity. Water comes from the well in the next village ten miles away.

Our country (China) has suffered another earthquake. Of our young people 60 per cent are displaced and have no homes. Many people have died or disappeared – probably buried! People are looking for their loved ones but are scared that the rubble will collapse. Communication links are down, there is no clean water and food is short.

My country, Uganda, is torn by civil war. It is terrible. Families are being torn apart – no one is spared. Our food supplies are affected by the fighting and not enough people to work in the fields. Many of our young men have been forced to fight, our girls have been raped and our houses destroyed. Our hospitals are damaged – many doctors and nurses are dead. People are homeless. The UN has set up refugee camps but they are badly in need of supplies.

My country, Ethiopia, is very poor. The levels of health care and education are low. We want to advance as a nation and compete in the world. Many of my people work hard and their produce is sold to dealers in other countries. They earn very little for this because trade is not fair and they haven't the business knowledge to improve. Often these cash crops mean that people here have very little to eat.

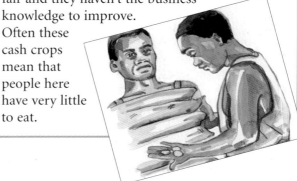

Charities

Buddhism

Tibet Foundation

History – Began in 1985 to create greater awareness of aspects of Tibetan Buddhism and the needs of the Tibetan people. Some of their activities are religious but they have worked to raise money and help for recent earthquakes and flood-affected areas.

Recent project – Bihar Floods. More than two thousand lives have been lost and thousands of others remain stranded without food, drinking water or basic necessities. Aid efforts were hampered by the limited access to more than 1800 villages suffering the impact of the floods across sixteen districts in Bihar State.

It is within this State that Bodhgaya is situated, the most sacred city for Tibetans and all Buddhists alike because Buddhism began here. The Tibet Foundation provided money and resources for the emergency relief effort.

Christianity ✝

CAFOD

History – This was set up in 1962. Historically, Catholic churches generated charity funds on one specific day of each year. They themselves decided what to do with this money. CAFOD was the organisation set up to centralise this fundraising, and be more effective and wide-ranging with it. Work which began as disaster relief and aid work now includes campaigning for a fairer world, and a vast array of educational work, including a schools magazine, as well as church magazines.

Recent project – Funding water pipes for a Brazilian shanty town to give access to clean water (this project gave the people belief in themselves and their ability to change their lives, as well as helping with health problems directly).

Hinduism ॐ

SEWA International

History – This is a UK charity, entirely run by dedicated volunteers from all sections of the community, working towards serving humanity. It funds long-term projects for economic development. It tries to combine modern and indigenous techniques to improve living conditions in affected disaster areas of India. It focuses on education, orphanages, village amenities and employment.

Recent project – Bihar Flood Appeal 2008. The floods were worse than expected; thousands died or were left homeless. Crops and cattle were destroyed. An appeal was set up to put projects in place to firstly give **emergency aid** and then set up projects that would build for the future to make people self sufficient.

The Basics

1 Give two reasons why the work of charities is important.
2 Why do you think religious people want to give to charity?
3 Why can charities not help everyone who asks?
4 Charities try to help people to help themselves. Why is this important?
5 **Charities should only help people of the same religion as they represent.** What do you think? Explain your answer

Islam ☪

Islamic Relief

<u>History</u> – Set up in 1984, and was the first Muslim relief agency in Europe providing humanitarian aid during emergency situations, and works for the long-term development of the world's poorest nations. It aims to try to alleviate the suffering of the needy wherever they are. The bulk of its development work is in Muslim countries.

<u>Recent projects</u> – One of the first agencies to send help to Bosnia, Albania and Chechnya. The Ramadan Package in 30 countries, including Pakistan and Kashmir, gives food parcels to the poor and needy. A free hospital and dispensary has been set up in Kashmir, whilst mobile health clinics are funded in Ingushetia.

All charities form a major part of the world's attempt to help the less fortunate. They fundraise throughout the year so that they are in a position to help when that help is required.

As well as this they are doing long-term work throughout the year, much of which goes unnoticed.

Judaism ✡

World Jewish Relief

<u>History</u> – World Jewish Relief was founded in 1933 to rescue Jews from the horrors taking place in Nazi Germany bringing 70,000 Jewish people to safety before the start of the Second World War. After the war, work began to respond to the needs of Jewish refugees and communities all over the world, with the aim of supporting Jews in distress. Its work involves empowering local communities, i.e. teaching them to be self-sufficient. Today WJR stands as the leading UK international agency responding to the needs of Jewish communities at risk or in crisis, outside the UK and Israel. At times of major international disaster, they lead the UK Jewish community's response to others in need all over the world.

<u>Recent project</u> – Since the break-up of the Soviet Union, many elderly Jews and orphans have been left behind, unsupported. Their living conditions, based on their state pensions, do not cover normal costs of basic living. WJR supports many through food provision and medical care. It also runs orphanages in the Ukraine, which take in street children.

Sikhism ☬

Khalsa Aid

<u>History</u> – Established in 1999, Khalsa Aid is an inter-national non-profit aid and relief organisation founded on the Sikh principles of selfless service and universal love. It is a UK registered charity and also has volunteers in North America and Asia. Khalsa Aid has provided relief assistance to victims of disasters, wars, and other tragic events around the world.

<u>Recent project</u> – The Punjab has seen heavy floods with thousands killed. Many villages have suffered immense economic hardship with the loss of basic living conditions. Over 134 villages, 11,080 hectares of standing crop and 55,000 people in Ferozpur have been affected. Khalsa Aid raised large sums of money for emergency aid, worked with governments to help refugees and tried to help rebuild the lives of many.

Task

Look at the work of the charity of the religion/s you are studying. Research this organisation in more depth using the internet or by contacting the charity itself – a speaker may attend one of your lessons. In groups of three or four create a presentation about the charity, focusing on the kind of work it is currently doing.

Now you know about charities

Types of aid

So what do we mean by aid? How is it organised and for what purposes? There are two types of aid: short-term and long-term.

What do you think is the difference?
Try writing down a definition for yourself.
Can you think of some examples for each one?

Short-term aid

Short-term aid means aid that is given when a disaster happens. It is the immediate response to a crisis like a flood or an earthquake. It is when people need the essentials to survive in the short term: medicine, food, clean water, tents and blankets. Often, charities join forces when things like this happen, firstly to raise money and secondly to distribute the goods. It is often the case that charities are already present in these countries because they have a history of natural disasters – so they are key to emergency responses. Governments often promise money and aid (USA and Britain usually respond fairly quickly) but they are not in a position to get it to the disaster areas. Often many of these places are war torn or have unco-operative governments and charities are often the best groups to negotiate these difficulties.

Asian tsunami, Indian flood, Burmese floods, China earthquake, Kenyan civil war

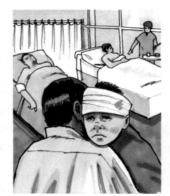

Once these have been put into action, **long-term aid** starts to rebuild lives of the survivors. It is really important to try to get people back into some kind of normal life. This helps them recover from the death of loved ones, destroyed homes and ruined livelihoods. To focus on recovery is to heal emotional wounds.

Task

The ideas below are examples of short-term aid that have been used over recent years. For each one, explain in what situation and how it might be used:

- sniffer dogs and specialist search teams
- RAF aircraft
- tents and refugee camps
- water cleaning tablets
- dehydration kits
- clearance teams.

The Basics

1 What does short-term aid mean?
2 Why are charities in a position to act so quickly when a disaster happens?
3 What is long-term aid?
4 Which is more important – short-term or long-term aid? Why?
5 **Sending food is no good because it runs out too quickly.** What do you think? Explain your answer.

Long-term aid

The key aim of long-term aid is to set up projects that will last and which the people of the country can manage. Examples of projects might be the building of schools and education programmes, hospital and medical projects and building wells for clean water in villages. The whole idea is to make the people have control of their own futures.

Gandhi, the great Indian leader, once said:

> *Give a man a fish and he can feed himself for a day; teach him how to use a fishing rod and he can feed himself forever.*

This statement really embodies the differences between the two types of aid.

Fact 1 – One in four people do not have access to safe water and hundreds die each day from dirty water.

There is a school located in Anuradhapura in Sri Lanka which had no electricity or running water. More families from the coastal areas arrived in town. The school could not cope with this growth. Long-term aid has provided an electric supply to the school and sufficient electricity to power a water pump to provide kitchen facilities and proper sanitation for the children and teachers.

Fact 2 – AIDS is killing hundreds of thousands in Africa.

In Uganda there are whole villages without adults because of HIV/AIDS. The Children of Uganda Charity is currently involved in Education and Food programmes. They have set up long-term sponsorship of children, orphanages (which are available until the age of 18) and national medical projects to inform about AIDS. They also, keep the profile of the charity high through people like the U2 band leader Bono.

Fact 3 – One–third of people in the developing world are totally illiterate. Around 77 million children do not go to school.

Millions of school-age children will never go to school. Millions more find themselves in overcrowded classrooms with untrained and underpaid teachers and no books or equipment.

Millions drop out of primary school before they get a basic education. Save The Children are setting up preschools and schools in refugee areas, providing qualified teachers and equipment.

 Now you know how long-term aid works

Sustainable development

This was defined by the UN's World Commission on Environment and Development as 'development that meets the needs of the present without compromising the ability of future generations to meet their needs'. In other words, growth and development must take place within the limits of ecological systems without major social and cultural disruption, and use technology that can be maintained locally. Ideally, the social, cultural, environmental and technological factors should be in balance.

From the environmental point of view, the local ecosystem should be able to support industries without damage from pollutants and waste. The natural resources of a country or area should be used carefully and not over-exploited and depleted. Industries should also be efficient in their use of energy.

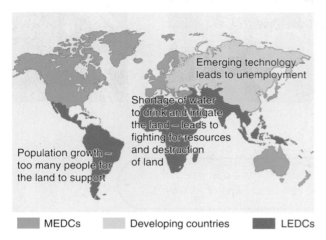

Problems of **sustainable development** in developing countries.

MEDCs   Developing countries   LEDCs

(Map labels: Emerging technology – leads to unemployment; Shortage of water to drink and irrigate the land – leads to fighting for resources and destruction of land; Population growth – too many people for the land to support)

Task

There are plenty of sustainable development projects across the world. Research one for yourself, or in pairs or in groups. Find out what the organisation does, current projects, how money is raised and how the volunteer system works. You could start with those mentioned on this page at: www.villagevolunteers.org and www.rainforestalliance.org.

Village Volunteers

Village Volunteers aims to improve life in villages. It is based upon the ideas of:

- Sustainable livelihood with social equality and justice.
- Economic growth.
- Health care and community development.
- Volunteer programmes.
- Women's rights.

The idea is to work in partnership with indigenous people to renew areas affected by poverty and disease, support cultural heritage and support achievement of their goals for the good of people and the environment.

Rainforest Alliance

As an independent, non-profit conservation organisation, the Rainforest Alliance works around the world to ensure that forestry, farming and tourism protect the environment and bring social and economic benefits to workers, their families and communities. Farms and forests that meet standards for sustainability earn the Rainforest Alliance Certified™ seal. These standards increase efficiency, reduce waste, minimise pesticide use and ensure that workers and their families have access to schools and medical care. The Rainforest Alliance involves businesses and consumers worldwide in the effort to bring responsibly produced goods and services to a global marketplace where the demand for sustainability is growing steadily.

Help, help, help, help!!!

Raise awareness

Sponsored events

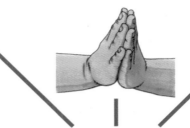

How can believers be a part of the sustainable development ideas and why should they care for others in poorer countries?

What can religious believers do about world poverty?

Time

Buy Fair Trade products

Exam Tips

Helpful hint – this question regarding how religious people can help in a given situation appears on exam papers regularly. You can use a pretty standard answer irrespective of what issue the question actually is. Firstly, with any problem religious people could pray, read their holy book, organise something at their local place of worship or raise awareness about the issue. Secondly, we have to remember that religious people are ordinary people and can respond in a way that is not specifically religious – by taking part in a sponsored event, giving time, giving money, buying products. If you learn these ideas it cuts down on how much you have to learn overall. You just have to use these ideas to relate to the actual question set.

Task

Explain how and why religious believers help those suffering from poverty.

Why do we help?

So, if all the above things happen when there is a disaster, or in a more long-term way, we must ask the question why? Why is it often the case that religious people (as well as many non-religious people) respond in a positive way? The answer goes back to the very first page of this topic. People with a sense of justice, equality and compassion respond when they see the suffering of others. Apparently a study has been done and it is thought that compassion is a uniquely human feeling. The animal kingdom does not have a response like this (although in a recent study of a group of African elephants and dolphins, some animal behaviour experts have noticed signs of compassion). However, if we stay with the human aspect of this, when we see images of suffering they spark in us a sense of sorrow and the desire to actually do something to help. We feel when we do help that we are doing something really worthwhile. This could be a simple action of donating money, or actually volunteering to give up time to help. For example, a doctor or a teacher may feel that to practise medicine or teach in a poor country is much more valuable than working in a hospital or school in their own rich country. This may be because they feel that their work is more appreciated and that they are really making a difference to the lives of those who have very little. To do something for others is a great act and there is the belief amongst religious people that they will find reward in the usage of their money – despair and suffering replaced by hope and smiles.

Now you know something about world poverty

Exam practice

AO2 questions

These are evaluative questions, and each full question will include two of these – one worth three marks and the other worth six marks. You have to do well on them, because they make up 50 per cent of the total mark. Let's check them out...

Evaluative questions always ask you what you think about something, or whether you agree. Actually, the exam isn't interested in whether you agree or not – it wants to know your reasoning. As long as you explain your reasons clearly, and you discuss the statement you were set, you should get marks.

Three-mark AO2 questions

These start with a statement, then say *What do you think? Explain your opinion.* The examiner is interested in your opinion – as long as it relates to the statement. You will get marks for making a couple of points and then explaining them, perhaps with an example to strengthen your argument. The exam watchdog (QCA) wants to see opportunities for you to give personal insights, and this is where you do that. Let's try a couple...

1 **It is God's will for some people to be poor.** What do you think? Explain your opinion.

2 **Religious people should always help the poor.** What do you think? Explain your answer.

Level 0	Unsupported opinion or no relevant evaluation.	0 marks
Level 1	Opinion (for example, I agree) supported by one simple reason.	1 mark
Level 2	Opinion supported by two simple reasons, or one elaborated reason.	2 marks
Level 3	Opinion supported by one well-developed reason, or a series of simple reasons, on one or both sides.	3 marks

Three mark questions always have a religious element stated in them. Although you can give your own personal insight, you have to make a response to the religious idea.

Getting used to the techniques of how to answer different types of questions reflectively is really important as well. Quite often good technique means you can answer more clearly and in a snappier style, which helps make it easy for the examiner to give you better marks!

Six-mark AO2 questions

OK for these you've got to do a whole lot more work. For a start, you will have to have some religion in there – maximum of three marks if you don't. Somewhere in the question there will be a prompt to remind you. Then you have to answer from two sides, in other words you have to agree <u>and</u> disagree, each time explaining your ideas – maximum of four marks if you don't.

So let's build from the three marker, because the first levels for these questions are the same. Let's try some...

3 **We should only help people in need in Britain, not around the world.** Do you agree? Give reasons for your answer, showing you have thought about more than one point of view. Refer to religious arguments in your answer.

4 **Helping the poor is a religious person's most important duty.** Do you agree? Give reasons for your answer, showing you have thought about more than one point of view.

Level 4	Opinion supported by two developed reasons, with reference to religion.	4 marks
Level 5	Evidence of reasoned consideration of two different points of view, with reference to religion.	5 marks
Level 6	A well-argued response, with evidence of reasoned consideration of two different points of view and clear reference to religion.	6 marks

Developed means you said something, and then explained it a bit.

Reasoned consideration just means 'some reasons with explanations'.

Revision outline

This a revision guide. It follows the outline of topics in the specification. If you already know all of the answers when you read through it, you will probably do brilliantly!

Use the guide as a checklist of what you know, and what you have still got to get to grips with. You could even use it as a last-minute check before you go into the exam. When you have finished all your revision, you should be able to recognise each word. Each phrase should trigger a whole lot of ideas in your head – definitions, examples, explanations. When it does, you are ready.

UNIT	WORDS TO LEARN	TOPICS WITHIN UNIT – DO YOU KNOW…?
ONE: RELIGIOUS ATTITUDES TO MATTERS OF LIFE (MEDICAL ETHICS)	Sanctity of life Medical research Human genetic engineering Embryology Cloning Stem cell therapy Transplant surgery Xenotransplantation Blood transfusion Experimentation Fertility treatment IVF AID AIH Surrogacy	• What religions believe about life • The benefits of medical research • The problems associated with medical research • Why (religious) people agree/disagree with human genetic engineering • Why (religious) people agree/disagree with embryo research • Why (religious) people agree/disagree with cloning • Why (religious) people agree/disagree with stem cell therapies • Why (religious) people agree/disagree with transplant surgery • The problems associated with xenotransplantation • Why (religious) people agree/disagree with blood transfusions • Why (religious) people want to have children • Why people need to use fertility treatment • Why (religious) people agree/disagree with IVF • Why (religious) people agree/disagree with AID/H • Why (religious) people agree/disagree with surrogacy • Whether any/all of these methods overstep the mark of 'playing God'

UNIT	WORDS TO LEARN	TOPICS WITHIN UNIT – DO YOU KNOW…?
TWO – RELIGIOUS ATTITUDES TO THE ELDERLY AND DEATH	Sanctity of life Quality of life Senior citizenship Ageism Retirement Care home Hospice Hospital Life-support machine Death Euthanasia Active euthanasia Passive euthanasia Life after death	• Why life is sacred/special • Why quality of life is important • The problems old people face • How families can support their elderly relatives • How the state supports old people • Why we should look after the elderly in society • What the law says about euthanasia • Whether it is OK to switch off life support • Whether life support is 'playing God' – in switching off or keeping on • Whether we should have the right to choose when we die • Who should be involved in decisions about death • The difference between active and passive euthanasia • Why some people want euthanasia • Why (religious) people agree/disagree with euthanasia • How (religious) people support the dying • Beliefs about life after death in at least one religion
THREE – RELIGIOUS ATTITUDES TO DRUG ABUSE	Mind Body Sanctity of life Medicine Legal drug Illegal drug Recreational drug Taxation Classification of drugs Rehabilitation	• Religious attitudes to the mind and body • What rights and responsibilities people have regarding drug use • Why (religious) people use drugs • The different types of drugs available – including their effect on the mind and body • The effects of legal drugs • Whether taxes should be used to fund medical research and treatment for drug users, including alcohol/tobacco-related illness • The problems associated with addiction • How (religious) people and society can help addicts and their families • The effectiveness of treatment and rehabilitation programmes • Why (religious) people and society should help addicts and their families • The law on drugs • Whether the laws relating to drugs are appropriate

UNIT	WORDS TO LEARN	TOPICS WITHIN UNIT – DO YOU KNOW…?
FOUR – RELIGIOUS ATTITUDES TO CRIME AND PUNISHMENT	Law Order Conscience Duty Responsibility Crime Punishment Crime against person Crime against property Crime against state Crime against religion Protection Retribution Deterrence Reformation Vindication Reparation Young offender Imprisonment Parole Capital punishment Tagging Probation Fines Community service Prison reform	• Religious attitudes to law and order • The concept of right and wrong • Responsibilities (religious) people have to follow the laws in a society • How conscience affects our behaviour • Why (religious) people commit crimes • What different types of crime there are, including examples of each • Why we punish people – the different aims of punishment • How punishment is matched to crime • How young offenders should be treated • How prisoners should be treated • The issues associated with life imprisonment • The issues associated with parole and early release • Why (religious) people agree/disagree with the death penalty • The alternatives to imprisonment, and how effective they are

UNIT	WORDS TO LEARN	TOPICS WITHIN UNIT – DO YOU KNOW…?
FIVE – RELIGIOUS ATTITUDES TO RICH AND POOR IN BRITISH SOCIETY	Rich Poor Money Wealth Poverty Charity Inheritance Wages Homelessness Apathy Gambling Addiction Counselling Minimum wage Excessive salary Responsibility Community Lottery	• Why people are rich in the UK • Why people are poor in the UK • The different ways in which personal wealth can be created • Religious attitudes to money • Religious attitudes to responsibility for the poor • Religious attitudes to the personal use of wealth • How (religious) people help the poor in the UK • Why (religious) people help the poor • How the state tries to help the poor in the UK • Whose actual responsibility it is to help the poor in the UK • Whether it is right to gamble • Whether it is right to gamble on the lottery • How lottery has created wealth in the UK
SIX – RELIGIOUS ATTITUDES TO WORLD POVERTY	Poverty LEDC Justice Stewardship Compassion Exploitation Debt Unfair trade Natural disaster War Global interdependence World trade Charity Emergency aid Long-term aid Sustainable development	• Religious attitudes to injustice • Religious attitudes to poverty • What is meant by justice, stewardship and compassion in the sense of world poverty • Why some countries are poor – the factors that have brought them/keep them at that level of poverty • Some examples of LEDCs • How global interdependence and world trade help/hinder attempts to help these countries • Why (religious) people help the poor in other countries • How (religious) people help the poor in other countries • The work of organisations in these countries • Why emergency aid is needed • The difference between emergency and long-term aid • Issues caused by these types of aid • Why sustainable development is needed, and its benefits

What a question paper looks like

You will be given a question paper and an answer booklet in the examination.

Do I really need to read the cover? It's always the same isn't it?

Well, no they aren't all the same, and it is easy in a stressful time to mix up what you are meant to do. Probably your teacher will have told you a million times what you have to do in the exam, but you can still forget. It is a good idea to just check through the cover – it is like a calming exercise which helps if you are nervous. It also reassures you that you do know what you are doing.

The cover will remind you:

- How long the exam lasts – so plan and use your time well. Reassess after each full question answered – you might have gained or lost time. Don't spend too much time on one question, but don't rush yourself either. You start with four questions to answer in 90 minutes – about 20–22 minutes a question.
- That you get a choice of any four of the six questions on offer. If you answer them all, you'll be given marks for the best four, but it might not be the best use of your time. Some people find they have lots of time left when they have finished what they should do, so they do extra questions to pass the time!
- That you can choose one or two religions for each question. If you have studied two religions, then it is a good idea to answer every question which asks for religious attitudes as if it was the same question twice, once for each religion. Your answer will be much clearer, and so easier to mark.
- To use blue or black ink/pen. This makes your paper easier to read and mark. This is especially important when exam papers are going to be

marked online – you need your writing to be clear and bold, so the examiner doesn't have to struggle to read it.
- That you should do any notes or practice work on either your answer booklet, or on extra paper. Sometimes, people write correct things that they then don't put into their real answer. If you hand in all your working out and notes, the examiner can credit you for anything you missed out. They are obliged to read it all. In your answer booklet, write on the lines only – don't go into the margins or above or below the box. The OMR system, which scans your booklet into the computer for the examiner to mark online, isn't designed to pick up anything outside the writing area – it might cost you marks.

So much for the cover, what about the inside?

There will be six questions, and the chances are that each one will have a picture or bit of writing to start with. The pictures are meant to stimulate your brain, and start you thinking. In other words, they are meant to help you by triggering the relevant ideas for that question.

In this sample paper, the questions are split 1/3/3/5/6. There has to be a 3- and a 6- mark evaluative, but the other nine marks could be split up a different way – could be 1/2/6, or 2/3/4, or 4/5, for example. So be prepared (through the practice in this book) for that.

Sample paper

If you answer all six, they will all be marked and your best four count.

Split into nine marks for knowledge, understanding and application, and nine marks for evaluation.

Choose any **four** questions from the six

Each question is worth **18 marks** in total

1 Religious Attitudes to Matters of Life (Medical Ethics)

Look at the picture below.

Image helps you with part a.

Don't confuse with AIH.

One mark per relevant reason.

(1.1) What is surrogacy?

(*1 mark*)

(1.2) Give **three** reasons why some religious people disagree with AID (Artificial Insemination by Donor)?

(*3 marks*)

(1.3) **Religious people should have children.** What do you think? Explain your opinion.

(*3 marks*)

You could give just one side in your response, but a two-sided answer is likely to be stronger.

You could talk about attitudes generally, or in one specific religion.

(1.4) Explain religious attitudes to embryo research. Refer to beliefs and teachings in your answer.

(*5 marks*)

(1.5) **Religious people should donate their organs after death**. Do you agree? Give reasons for your answer, showing you have thought about more than one point of view.

(*6 marks*)

Remember DREARER!

2   Religious Attitudes to the Elderly and Death

It is only one mark, so just write one sentence.

(2.1)   What is a hospice?   (*1 mark*)

This means make them feel better, not cure them.

(2.2)   Give **three** ways in which religious people can comfort the dying.   (*3 marks*)

(2.3)   **There is no such thing as life after death**. What do you think?
          Explain your answer.   (*3 marks*)

If you answer from the perspective of two religions, it will be easier to reach 5 marks.

(2.4)   Explain religious attitudes to the elderly. Refer to beliefs and teachings in
          your answer.   (*5 marks*)

(2.5)   **Euthanasia (mercy killing) is murder**. Do you agree? Give reasons for your answer,
          showing you have thought about more than one point of view. Refer to religious
          arguments in your answer.   (*6 marks*)

Remember DREARER!

3   Religious Attitudes to Drug Abuse

Get the right kind in your answer.

Key word – get this wrong and you'll get no marks.

(3.1)   Name an illegal drug.   (*1 mark*)

(3.2)   Give **three** reasons why some people use illegal drugs.   (*3 marks*)

(3.3)   **Religious believers should support drug rehabilitation programmes**. What do you think? Explain your opinion.   (*3 marks*)

(3.4)   Explain religious attitudes to the mind and body. Refer to beliefs and teachings in your answer.   (*5 marks*)

(3.5)   **Alcohol should be made illegal**. Do you agree? Give reasons for your answer, showing you have thought about more than one point of view. Refer to religious arguments in your answer.   (*6 marks*)

4   Religious Attitudes to Crime and Punishment

You need to show some religious arguments in your answer. This reminds you because the question statement isn't automatically pointing you to giving that information.

This means <u>why</u> we punish.

(4.1)   What is meant by *conscience*?   (*1 mark*)

(4.2)   Give **three** aims of punishment.   (*3 marks*)

(4.3)   **Religious people are wrong to say you should forgive murderers**. What do you think? Explain your opinion.   (*3 marks*)

(4.4)   Explain religious attitudes to capital punishment (death penalty). Refer to beliefs and teachings in your answer.   (*5 marks*)

(4.5)   **Young offenders should never be imprisoned**. Do you agree? Give reasons for your answer, showing you have thought about more than one point of view. Refer to religious arguments in your answer.   (*6 marks*)

5   **Religious Attitudes to Rich and Poor in British Society**

More millionaires in UK than ever before

UNEMPLOYMENT SET TO REACH 3 MILLION

'There is real poverty in this country' says MP

(5.1) What is the *Lotto*?   (*1 mark*)

(5.2) Explain why some people gamble.   (*3 marks*)

(5.3) **All wealth comes from God**. What do you think? Explain your opinion.   (*3 marks*)

(5.4) Explain, using beliefs and teachings, why religious people help the poor.   (*5 marks*)

(5.5) **Religious people should support the minimum wage**. Do you agree? Give
       reasons for your answer, showing you have thought about more than one
       point of view.   (*6 marks*)

> This means two sides – agree and disagree (with reasons and explanations) and at least one religious argument.

6   **Religious Attitudes to World Poverty**

(6.1) What is meant by *compassion*?   (*1 mark*)

(6.2) Explain why some countries are very poor.   (*3 marks*)

> Can give one side or two sides on these three mark questions.

(6.3) **All Religious believers should give money to charity.** What do you think?
       Explain your opinion.   (*3 marks*)

(6.4) Explain how religious believers might treat people in LEDCs (Less Economically
       Developed Countries)?   (*5 marks*)

(6.5) **Helping the poor is the most important duty for a religious believer**. Do you agree?
       Give reasons for your answer, showing you have thought about more than one
       point of view.   (*6 marks*)

> If it is a technical term, the exam paper usually writes it out in brackets to help you.

Glossary

Active euthanasia mercy killing (euthanasia) where the patient is killed before the illness kills them

Ageism prejudice against someone because of their age, leading to discrimination

AID/H Artificial Insemination by Donor/Husband (type of fertility treatment)

Blood transfusion medical procedure where blood is replaced within the body, either because of loss of blood through an accident, or in an operation

Caffeine stimulant drug found in coffee, tea and other drinks

Capital punishment the death penalty; state execution where the prisoner is put to death for the crime(s) they have committed

Care home for the elderly home where elderly people go to live, and where they can be looked after

Charity giving to the needy. Charity organisations do not work for profits, but (usually) to help others

Classification of drugs the legal system which classifies illegal drugs into Class A, B or C

Cloning the scientific method by which animals or plants can be copied exactly to create an identical new being, because the DNA of the original has been used

Community service punishment whereby the offender has to work for between 60 and 240 hours serving the community

Compassion loving kindness; helping others with no desire for reward

Conscience sense of right and wrong, often thought of as good/bad voices in the head which guide your behaviour

Crime action which breaks the law

Death end of life; when there is no longer any brain stem activity, and organs cease to function on their own

Designer babies babies whose DNA has been modified to ensure they have specific characteristics

Deterrence punishment to make the offender or others not repeat the crime

Drug abuse misuse of drugs, often so that it has serious, negative side effects

Duty the role someone has; what they have to do

Electronic tagging punishment; anklet which tracks the movement of offender, so that they can be monitored

Embryology study of and research using embryos

Emergency aid aid which is given in emergency situations, for example, after a natural disaster

Euthanasia mercy killing; helping someone to die to ease suffering, out of compassion and with their agreement

Excessive salaries term given to salaries which most people think are too big for the job done

Experimentation scientific way of checking and proving hypotheses (in this book it is related to medical experiments on humans)

Exploitation misuse of power/money to get others to do things for little/unfair reward

Fair trade trade in which the producer gets a fair return for their work/produce

Fertility treatment medical treatment to aid fertility

Fines where the offender has to pay money as their punishment

Gambling placing of money on an uncertain outcome to win more money back

Global interdependence the idea that countries depend on other countries around the world and are themselves depended on

Homelessness the status of having nowhere to live

Hospice a place for the dying, where they can have dignity whilst they die

Hospital a place where people are treated for illness and accident

Human genetic engineering modification of genetic make-up (DNA) to change the features of a human

Illegal drugs drugs which are not legal, for example, heroin, cocaine

Imprisonment punishment in which an offender is locked up in jail for a period of time

Inheritance money gained from family death

IVF in vitro fertilisation; fertility treatment resulting in 'test tube babies'

Justice fairness; what is right; making up for wrongs done

Law and order justice system which helps support good behaviour in society by punishing bad behaviour

LEDC Less Economically Developed Country

Life after death religious beliefs about what happens when we die

Life-support machine machine which keeps a person alive when their own organs are unable to do so

Long-term aid aid which is long lasting, and designed to continue without total external support, for example, building of a medical centre

Lotto national lottery game in the UK; a form of gambling

Medical research research which is designed to lead to medical advances, and so improve medical treatment

Minimum wage the legal minimum an employer can pay to an employee

Parole punishment; where a prisoner is released from prison, and is still monitored through the parole service for a set period

Passive euthanasia mercy killing; euthanasia whereby medicines/treatment are removed so that the person will die more quickly from their illness

Poverty condition of being without money, food, shelter and other basic needs of life

Prison reform changes made to prisons to improve their potential to look after and rehabilitate offenders

Probation punishment whereby an offender is monitored for a set period of time

Protection aim of punishment, which makes sure others are safe from the offender

Punishment what is done to a person because they have committed a crime

Quality of life measure of fulfilment; how good life is

Recreational drugs drugs which are taken in social settings, for example, alcohol

Reformation aim of punishment, which is to make someone a better person, understanding what they did was wrong and why it was

Rehabilitation procedure to support drug addicts/prisoners back into society as normal members of society, and not going back to previous behaviours

Reparation aim of punishment whereby the offender is making up for what they have done; paying back

Responsibility the thing(s) which we have to look after

Retirement ending working life

Retribution aim of punishment; to get revenge

Sanctity of life idea that life is special or sacred

Saviour sibling baby born, perhaps with modified DNA, to become a donor for a sibling and so save/improve their life

Senior citizen person over a certain age (65)

Stem cell therapy medical treatment which uses stem cells from embryos to treat conditions such as Parkinson's disease

Stewardship idea that humans have a duty to look after the world

Surrogacy where one woman becomes pregnant and carries the pregnancy to full term in order to hand the baby over when born to another woman for its upbringing

Sustainable development development which will be sustainable, i.e. keep going, and not be limited by time/money/environmental issues

Taxation a portion of the cost of items which goes to the government; also taxation on wages

Therapeutic cloning use of DNA and cells to create a replica organ for use in medical research, medical treatment and transplant surgery

Transplant surgery medical treatment to replace faulty/damaged/useless organs and hence improve life for someone

Vindication aim of punishment whereby the breaking of the law must be shown to be respected by applying a punishment to the offender

Wealth having sufficient money/possessions for a good life

World trade trade between countries in the world

Young offender person under the age of eighteen who has committed a crime

Index